Pocket
PHUKET

TOP SIGHTS • LOCAL LIFE • MADE EASY

D1024624

Isabella Noble

In This Book

QuickStart Guide

Your keys to understanding the city – we help you decide what to do and how to do it

Need to Know
Tips for a smooth trip

Regions
What's where

Explore Phuket

The best things to see and do, neighbourhood by neighbourhood

Top Experiences
Make the most of your visit

Local Life
The insider's city

The Best of Phuket

The city's highlights in handy lists to help you plan

Best Walks
See the city on foot

Phuket's Best...
The best experiences

Survival Guide

Tips and tricks for a seamless, hassle-free city experience

Getting Around
Travel like a local

Essential Information
Including where to stay

Our selection of the region's best places to eat, drink and experience:

◎ **Sights**

✖ **Eating**

🍷 **Drinking**

★ Entertainment

🛍 **Shopping**

These symbols give you the vital information for each listing:

🖉 Telephone Numbers		👪	Family-Friendly
⊙ Opening Hours		🐾	Pet-Friendly
P Parking		🚌	Bus
⊖ Nonsmoking		🚢	Ferry
@ Internet Access		Ⓜ	Metro
📶 Wi-Fi Access		🚋	Tram
🥗 Vegetarian Selection		🚆	Train
📖 English-Language Menu			

Find each listing quickly on maps for each neighbourhood:

Bar Hemingway

16 🍷 Map p233, B2

Legend has it that Hemi
self, wielding a machine
rate this timber-pan
ered bar during
showpiece is a
en by Papa ar
town. Dress
s.com; Hôtel Rit
⊙6.30pm-2a

6 ◎ Plac

Lonely Planet's Phuket

Lonely Planet Pocket Guides are designed to get you straight to the heart of the region.

Inside you'll find all the must-see sights, plus tips to make your visit to each one really memorable. We've split Phuket into easy-to-navigate regions and provided clear maps so you'll find your way around with ease. Our expert author has searched out the best of Phuket: walks, food, nightlife and shopping, to name a few. Because you want to explore, our 'Local Life' pages will take you to some of the most exciting areas to experience the real Phuket.

And of course you'll find all the practical tips you need for a smooth trip: itineraries for short visits, how to get around, and how much to tip the guy who serves you a drink at the end of a long day's exploration. It's your guarantee of a really great experience.

Our Promise

You can trust our travel information because Lonely Planet authors visit the places we write about, each and every edition. We never accept freebies for positive coverage, so you can rely on us to tell it like it is.

QuickStart Guide 7

Explore Phuket 21

Worth a Trip:

The Best of Phuket 123

Phuket's Best Walks

Phuket's Best ...

Survival Guide 143

QuickStart Guide

Welcome to Phuket

The original island getaway, Phuket may be older, pricier and much less undiscovered these days, but it still has that special allure. The pure-white beaches, psychedelic sunsets and aquamarine sea, they're all here, and Phuket continues to party in style. It may be too popular for its own good, but that's what happens when you've got it all.

Phuket
Top Experiences

Big Buddha (p92)

You've seen him peeking out from different angles all over the island, but taking in the sheer size of Phuket's 45m Big Buddha up close makes for a worthy break from the beach.

Laem Phromthep (p72)

Watch the sun sink into the sparkly Andaman Sea, blazing the sky a deep-red orange or hot pink, from the island's southernmost cape and most loved viewpoint.

Diving in the Similan Islands (p120)

Uncover the majestic underwater paradise of Thailand's most famous dive spot, where you'll be enchanted by everything from perfect turquoise water to tiny plume worms and majestic whale sharks.

Day-Trippin' Ko Phi-Phi (p114)

With its lush blonde beaches, azure seas and tumbling jungle, it's no wonder Phi-Phi is a popular day trip from Phuket. Dive, hike, laze on bright-white sands or boat around beautiful Phi-Phi Leh.

ck Climbing in Railay, Krabi (p116)

abi's trademark karst formations curve along the white-fringed coast like a
nt limestone fortress in laid-back Railay. Embark on the ultimate jungle-gym
venture rock climbing up high.

Hidden Hôrng of Ao Phang-Nga (p118)

Sea kayak through one of the Andaman's most dramatic landscapes, past soaring limestone towers, craggy cliffs, shimmering sea and peaceful *hôrng* (semi-submerged island lagoons), in ridiculously beautiful Ao Phang-Nga.

Phuket
Local Life

Insider tips to help you find the real Phuket

There are plenty of ways to enrich your visit when you tire of beaching around. No Phuket trip is complete without exploring Phuket Town's old-world charms and, at least, glimpsing the madness of Patong's local nightlife.

A Wander Around the Old Town (p24)

▶ Converted Sino-Portuguese shophouses
▶ Chinese Taoist shrines

Phuket Town is your window into Phuket's historical and cultural soul. Spend at least a day wandering streets packed with incense-cloaked shrines and revamped Sino-Portuguese shophouses, where generations-old eateries mix with quirky galleries, guesthouses and boutiques.

Pub & Grub Crawl Patong (p40)

▶ Seafood stalls
▶ Fun-filled bars

Tourism-dominated Patong doesn't have much 'local' flavour, but it certainly flaunts its own character. Experience it on a pub tour of booze spots that dodge the seedy 'sin city' feel, debunking the myth that Patong is entirely about girly bars.

STEPHEN J BOITANO / GETTY IMAGES ©

Nightlife in Hat Patong (p38)

Food stall, Hat Patong (p38)

Other great places to experience the region like a local:

Wat Chalong (p77)

Phuket Town's Markets (p36)

Rawai's Seafood Grills (p80)

Wat Karon (p60)

Wat Suwan Khiri Wong (p46)

Masjid Mukaram Bang Thao (p85)

Phuket Town's Sino-Portuguese Architecture (p28)

Phuket
Day Planner

Day One

Spend your first morning switching into Phuket mode with a massage and coffee scrub at Kata's indulgent **Baray Spa** (p60). Beat the heat by whizzing up to **Big Buddha** (p92) early, taking a couple of hours to explore and drink in the spectacular views you've been longing for. Then grab a cheap, classic Thai lunch at **Pad Thai Shop** (p64) in Karon and an espresso at Kata's **Italian Job** (p68).

Start afternoon one of beach lazing on gorgeous **Hat Kata Yai** (p60) or head south to more secluded casuarina-fringed **Hat Nai Han** (p75). As the sun starts to sink, wind your way to **Laem Phromthep** (p72) to soak up the blazing sunset and unbeatable views. Drop down to chilled-out **Nikita's** (p80) on Hat Rawai or swing by **After Beach Bar** (p67) for cold beers and more dreamy Andaman Sea panoramas en route back to Kata.

Splash out on dinner overlooking white sands at Kata's wonderfully romantic **Boathouse Wine & Grill** (p64). Hold off on Patong, for now, and round the evening off with relaxing cocktails at beachside **Ska Bar** (p66) or eccentric **Mr Pan's Art Space** (p67) instead.

Day Two

Today you're off to explore Phuket Town's rich history. Kick off with breakfast at **Gallery Cafe** (p32) or keep it traditional at **Abdul's Roti Shop** (p24), before meandering around the Old Town's majestic Sino-Portuguese mansions and colourfully restored shophouses. If you fancy local insight, join a guided walk with **Phuket Heritage Trails** (p27).

While you're here, savour refined Royal Thai cooking at **Blue Elephant** (p31). Hang around for a cooking class to master all those fantastic recipes, then pick up a latte at coolly contemporary **Bo(ok)hemian** (p35) and detour to tucked-away boutiques and galleries, such as **Ranida** (p36), **Ban Boran Textiles** (p36) and **Drawing Room** (p37).

If you're keen for more of Phuket Town, enjoy world-class Thai fusion food at **Suay** (p31) and hit locally loved pub-club **Timber Hut** (p34). Otherwise, head back west to **Hat Kata Noi** (p60) and freshen up for a swanky, Mediterranean dining experience at **Mom Tri's Kitchen** (p64). Afterwards, catch a *moo·ay tai* (Thai boxing; also *muay Thai*) bout at Patong's **Bangla Boxing Stadium** (p52) or finish up with Chalong Bay Rum mojitos at **La Gritta** (p48).

hort on time?

Ve've arranged Phuket's must-sees into these day-by-day itineraries to make sure
ou see the very best of the region in the time you have available.

Day Three

☀ Wake up and smell the espresso at **Bocconcino** (p88), just inland rom **Hat Surin** (p85). Wander Surin's elegant boutiques for Phuket treats, such s beach-chic fashion from **Chandra** (90), all-natural beauty products from **emongrass House** (p90) or art from **Oriental Fine Art** (p90). Spend the rest f the morning lazing in luxury at **Catch Beach Club** (p85) and tuck into the tasty Thai-international lunches here.

☀ Next, head around the corner to beautiful **Laem Singh** (p85) nd continue south to chilled-out **Hat Kamala** (p85) to see the **Tsunami Mem orial** (p85) and for more beach lounging. Refuel with a luscious tropical juice at Kamala's sand-side **Meena Restaurant** (p87) and, if you're visiting during the monsoon, take a surfing class.

☾ Hopefully, you've prebooked show tickets for Patong's glit-ery **Phuket Simon Cabaret** (p52) xtravaganza, but first treat yourself to a glamorous candlelit Thai dinner at **Baan Rim Pa** (p47). Then it's time to hit the Patong party scene to see what the fuss s about. Do a pub crawl and pack onto he dancefloor at **Seduction** (p50) or **Illuzion** (p50).

Day Four

☀ Start early with a visit to the **Phuket Gibbon Rehabilitation Project** (p103) in the island's northeast, where you'll hear the gibbons' distinctive morning song. Swing by **Monkeypod** (p105) for delicious coffee en route. Wander upriver to **Nam Tok Bang Pae** (p104), relishing the refreshing natural beauty of **Khao Phra Thaew Royal Wildlife & Forest Reserve** (p103), then make time to admire Phuket's semi-submerged golden Buddha at **Wat Phra Thong** (p104).

☀ Travel west to lush Ao Bang Thao for a late lunch at **Bliss Beach Club** (p98), before relaxing the afternoon away on its plush deck and strolling along beautiful **Hat Bang Thao** (p97) out the front. If you can tear yourself away, pop inland for a massage at **Thai Carnation** (p97).

☾ Come dinner time, head 2km inland to enjoy ambitious, creative Thai-international cooking at **Bampot** (p97) or perhaps a bit of jazz at **Siam Supper Club** (p98). And while you're all glammed up, keep it classy with beach-front drinks late into the night at **Xana Beach Club** (p97).

Need to Know

For more information,
see Survival Guide (p143)

Currency
Thai baht (B)

Language
Thai

Visas
Generally not required for stays of up to 30
days when arriving by air.

Money
ATMs widely available. Credit cards
accepted in most hotels and restaurants.

Mobile Phones
Local SIM cards are readily available at
shopping centres and convenience stores
such as 7-Eleven, and work with any
unlocked GSM phone.

Time
Thailand Standard Time (GMT/UTC plus
seven hours)

Plugs & Adaptors
Outlets usually take European round two-
pronged pins and US flat two-pronged pins.
Electrical current is 220V.

Tipping
Tips of 5% to 10% for service workers are
greatly appreciated. A 10% service charge
is usually included on bills at high-end
establishments.

① Before You Go

Your Daily Budget

Budget: less than 1800B
► Dorm bed 250–500B
► Market or street stall *pàt tai* 40B
► Inexpensive public transport 25–50B

Midrange: 1800–7000B
► Midrange hotel room 1000–3000B
► Two-course dinner with drink 600–1000B
► Massage at a reputable spa 400–800B

Top end: more than 7000B
► Luxury beachfront resort room
6500–30,000B
► Degustation menu at a top restaurant
1300–5000B
► Lavish treatment at an exclusive spa
2000–7000B

Useful Websites

► **Lonely Planet** (www.lonelyplanet.com/
thailand/phuket-province) Destination information, hotel bookings, traveller forum.

► **Jamie's Phuket** (www.jamie-monk.blog
spot.com) Fun, insider's blog by a long-time
Phuket expat; excellent tips.

► **Phuket.com** (www.phuket.com)
Sophisticated compendium of island-wide
information.

Advance Planning

Two months before If travelling in high
season, book your hotel, and enquire about
cycling, walking and kayaking tours.

Two weeks before Book tickets for Phuket
Simon Cabaret.

One week before Book in for a day at a
beach club.

2 Arriving in Phuket

Phuket International Airport (Map p108; 076 327230; www.phuketairportthai.com) 30km northwest of Phuket Town. Metered taxis (500B to 700B to most beaches) are Om to the right as you exit arrivals. An airport bus (www.airportbusphuket.com) runs Phuket Town (100B, one hour).

From Phuket International Airport

Destination	Best Transport
Hat Kamala & Hat Surin	Private or metered taxi
Hat Karon & Hat Kata	Private or metered taxi
Hat Patong	Private or metered taxi
Phuket Town	Airport bus
Rawai	Private or metered taxi

At the Airport

Phuket International Airport There are TMs and currency exchanges here. You can arrange car hire from a number of car-rental agencies, including **Hertz** (076 328545; www.hertz.com; 8am-9pm) and **Avis** (02 251 1131; www.avis.com; 7am-pm), outside the arrivals hall. The airport osts a duty-free store, as well as a tourist nformation counter and postal facilities.

3 Getting Around

Transport on Phuket is much pricier than in other parts of Thailand. Despite the governing military's recent improvement efforts, at the time of writing, metered taxis remain hard to find beyond the airport, while private taxis and túk-túk charge exorbitant (if now more restricted) prices.

Private Taxi

An easy way to get around is to hire wheels with a driver and air-con. It's a good option for exploring the island on a day trip and particularly cost-effective for several people together. You'll find obvious taxi ranks in beach towns; most travel agents arrange drivers.

Túk-Túk

Plying the coastal routes between beach towns, this local mode of transport is pricey but convenient for getting from A to B. Handy if you're splitting costs between a group.

Car & Motorcycle Rental

The best way to get around is with your own wheels. Scooters can be hired everywhere (250B to 300B), but be aware of risks; there are high rates of accidents. Car rental is a safer option and can be arranged from Phuket Town, the airport and most beach areas (from 1200B).

Sŏrng·tǎa·ou (Passenger Pick-Up Truck)

An inexpensive local-style way to get to the beaches from Phuket Town, but only an option if you aren't in a rush.

Boat

Chartering a long-tail or speedboat is a convenient way to visit outlying islands, particularly from Rawai.

Phuket
Regions

Ao Bang Thao (p94)
A stunning 8km stretch of blinding-white sand with a sprinkling of resorts and beach clubs along the southern half, and some stellar restaurants tucked inland.

Hat Kamala & Hat Surin (p82)
Sophisticated Hat Surin and its slightly more laid-back neighbour, Hat Kamala, manage to mix beach bliss with a village vibe.

Hat Patong (p38)
Go-go bars, raunchy cabaret, pounding nightclubs and hedonism at every turn: Patong is Phuket's 'sin city' and proud of it.

Hat Karon & Hat Kata (p56)
Perfect for families, Kata offers high-end dining, beachside bars and beautiful beaches, while Karon has a gorgeous, long white-sand stretch.

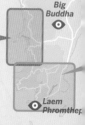

Big Buddha

Laem Phromthep

Northern Beaches (p106)

If you're after quiet-ish, more natural beaches, head north to these beauties that have managed to escape the full effects of the tourism boom...for now.

Thalang & Around (p100)

Hike to waterfalls, zip-line through lush jungle, explore majestic wát and meet singing gibbons in Khao Phra Thaew Royal Wildlife & Forest Reserve.

Phuket Town & Around (p22)

Century-old Sino-Portuguese shophouses, Chinese Taoist temples, boutique guesthouses, art galleries and lively bars are just some of many reasons to fall for Phuket's cultural capital.

Rawai (p70)

Discover spectacular viewpoints, chilled-out bars, secluded sands in hidden pockets and a whole new mellow vibe in breezy, low-key Rawai.

⊙ Top Experiences

Laem Phromthep

Worth a Trip

⊙ Top Experiences

Big Buddha

Ko Phi-Phi

Railay, Krabi

Ao Phang-Nga

Similan Islands

Explore
Phuket

Worth a Trip

Hat Patong

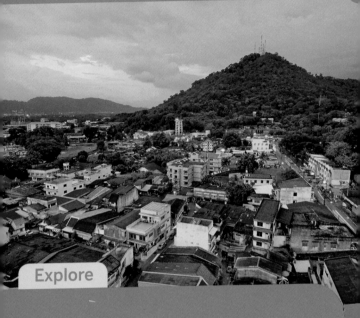

Explore

Phuket Town & Around

What, no beaches? Trade roasting in the sun for soaking up local culture in Phuket's most authentic corner. Peek down alleyways to serene incense-shrouded Chinese Taoist shrines and wander the lantern-strewn streets aglow at night. Sino-Portuguese *hôrng tăa·ou* (shophouses) huddle together, hosting artsy cafes, inexpensive boutique-chic guesthouses, quirky galleries and buzzing bars, which attract a mixed, fashionable crowd of Thais, expats and tourists.

The Region in a Day

 Fuel up on omelettes and breakfast bagels at **Gallery Cafe** (p32), then take in the old-style charm and historical Sino-Portuguese buildings of Phuket Town's streets. Put it all into context at **Phuket Thaihua Museum** (p27), before swinging by **Chyn Pracha House** (p27). Jump in a taxi to **Khao Rang** (p27) for city panoramas, shade and fresh air. If you're feeling active, brave the one-hour walk back to town. Hungry yet? Drop into **The Cook** (p32) for green-chicken-curry pizza.

Devote your afternoon to practising royal culinary skills at **Blue Elephant Cooking School** (p28). Otherwise, grab an Americano and a good read at **Bo(ok)hemian** (p35) and stock up on upmarket vintage fashion at **Ranida** (p36), affordable fabrics and accessories at **Ban Boran Textiles** (p36), or colourful abstract art at **Drawing Room** (p37).

Dine in fusion-tastic style at **Suay** (p31) or enjoy simpler classics at **Raya** (p32), before falling into a cartoon-covered beer and cocktail world at **Comics** (p35). Once things get rowdier, move on to live music at **Rockin' Angels** (p35) or hit **Timber Hut** (p34) for pub-club dancing to pure-pop favourites.

For a local's day in Phuket Town, see p24.

 Local Life

A Wander Around the Old Town

 Best of Phuket Town

Drinking & Nightlife

Timber Hut (p34)

Comics (p35)

Bo(ok)hemian (p35)

Rockin' Angels (p35)

Dining

Suay (p31)

Blue Elephant (p31)

Gallery Cafe (p32)

Raya (p32)

Getting There

🚕 **Taxi** Costs 550B to/from the airport.

Airport Bus Bright-orange airport buses (100B, one hour) run to/from Phuket Town from 6.30am to 8.30pm.

Túk-túk Charters cost 500B to 600B between the west-coast tourist beaches and Phuket Town.

Sŏrng·tăa·ou These passenger pick-up trucks ply the routes from Phuket Town's Th Ranong to the west-coast beach towns (30B to 40B), but take hours.

Local Life
A Wander Around the Old Town

The most rewarding way to explore Phuket Town is a slow stroll around the core Old Town, where history seeps through the cracks at every turn. This itinerary takes in some of the Sino-Portuguese relics housing generations-old businesses and restaurants, passing shrines pocketed away in narrow alleys and unveiling local markets and popular delicacies.

1 Traditional Roti

Breakfast with a bang: time to devour famously delicious roti at **Abdul's Roti Shop** (Th Thalang; dishes 30B; ◷7am-4pm Mon-Sat, 7am-noon Sun). A 70-plus-year-old immigrant, Abdul has been cooking flaky roti on the street outside his shop for years. Whether you're a sweet or savoury lover, this place has it covered, with sticky banana roti or plain roti with spicy chicken, beef or fish massaman curry.

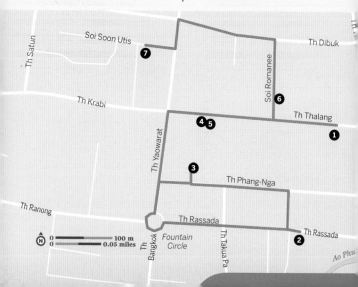

2 Thavorn Hotel

Opened in 1961 by the tin-mining Chinese-Thai Thavorn Wong Wongse family, the **Thavorn** (www.thavornhotel. com; 74 Th Rassada; museum admission 30B; museum 9am-4pm) was Phuket's original five-star and one of the oldest hotels still operating. The facade is unimpressive, but the wood-panelled memorabilia-packed interior is a vintage throwback with a grand wooden staircase leading off the lobby. The dusty museum has tin toys, old movie projectors and historical photos.

3 Shrine of the Serene Light

A handful of Chinese temples pump colour into Phuket Town, but this restored **shrine** (Saan Jao Sang Tham; Th Phang-Nga; admission free; 8.30am-noon & 1.30-5.30pm), tucked away up a 50m alley, is particularly atmospheric, with Taoist etchings on the walls, the vaulted ceiling stained from incense plumes and an altar that's always fresh with flowers and burning candles. The shrine is said to have been built by a local family in the 1890s.

4 Oldest Herbs Shop

You can't miss the wafting aromas of the **Oldest Herbs Shop** (099 359 9564; Th Thalang; 7.30am-6pm Mon-Sat, 7.30-11.30am Sun), genuinely Phuket's oldest, as you stroll down Th Thalang. Stock up on Chinese-origin remedies or simply admire portions of herbs being weighed on antique scales and mixed together ready for sale at this generations-old family business.

5 Kopitiam by Wilai

For inexpensive local-style feasting, **Kopitiam by Wilai** (083 606 9776; www. facebook.com/kopitiambywilai; 18 Th Thalang; mains 80-120B; 11am-10pm Mon-Sat;) serves Phuket soul food. It does Phuketian *pàt tai* (thin rice noodles with egg, tofu and/or shrimp) with a kick, and a fantastic *mee sua*: noodles sautéed with egg, greens, prawns, chunks of sea bass, and squid. Finish off with fresh chrysanthemum or passionfruit juice.

6 Soi Romanee

Once home to brothels, gamblers and opium dens, modern-day Soi Romanee is as wonderfully saccharine as a street can get. Squeezed between Th Thalang and Th Dibuk, this alley is lined with restored Sino-Portuguese shophouses in vivid pastels, transformed into boutique guesthouses. It's particularly beautiful at night, when coloured-paper Chinese lanterns cast a soft glow. You'll often catch wedding photo shoots in action.

7 Cookie House

There's no sign, but on the south side of tranquil Soi Soon Utis you'll find **Cookie House** (087 885 9538, 076 213010; Soi Soon Utis; 7am-9pm). The young matriarch of this Sino-Portuguese shophouse makes fabulous cookies from freshly pulverised almond paste, egg yolks and butter. Whether you go sweet, salty or mixed, consider these crumbly treats in white boxes a Phuketian delicacy.

Khao
Rang 3

11

Th Chumphon

Phuket Bus
Terminal 2
(3km)

Th Damrong

Th Thungkha

Th Mae Luan

Th Yaowarat

22

Th Thepkasattri

Th Suthat

Th Na

Raintree
Spa 6

Th Satun

Th Dibuk

Th Patipat

Phuket
Heritage
Trails 4

20

Th Dibuk

Th Dibuk

16

Limelight Av

Th Lu
Phav

Chyn
Pracha 5 7
House

2

Th Yaowarat

Soi
Romanee

24

28

Tourism
Authority of
Thailand Office

Th Krabi

Blue
Elephant Thaihua
Cooking Museum
School

15

25

Th Thalang

Phuket
Sealand Co

12

Th Lua
Phav

34

17

18

14 33

Phuket
Termir
(200

Jui Tui
Shrine 8

Th Ranong

13

32

30

Th Phang-Nga

Th Phang-Nga

23

29

Fountain
Circle

21

Sŏrng·tăa·ou
to beaches

31

19

26

Th Rassada

Th Chao Fa West

Soi Puthorn

Suay
Cooking
School

1

Th Takua Pa

Ao Phuket

Th Phuket

Th Phuket

Soi Surin

Th Montri

27

10

Weekend
Market
(700m)

Th Bangkok

Th Taling Chan

Th Thlok Uthit

Soi 9

Th Ong
Sim Phai

Bang
Niew 9
Shrine
Phuket
Immigration
Office (600m)

Th Kra

For reviews see	
⊙ Experiences	p27
✕ Eating	p31
⊖ Drinking	p34
✪ Entertainment	p36
⚿ Shopping	p36

N 0   400 m
   0   0.2 miles

Experiences

Suay Cooking School
COOKING COURSE

1 Map p26, C4

Learn from one of Phuket's top chefs at the most laid-back, soulful and fun cooking school around. Noy Tammasak will lead you through the local market and teach you how to make three dishes, before cracking open a bottle of wine to enjoy with your creations. Minimum three people. (☎081 797 4135; www.suayrestaurant.com; 50/2 Th Takua Pa; per person 1800B)

Phuket Thaihua Museum
MUSEUM

2 Map p26, B3

Formerly a Chinese language school, this flashy museum is filled with photos and English-language exhibits on Phuket's history, from the Chinese migration (many influential Phuketian families are of Chinese origin) and the tin-mining era to local cuisine, fashion and literature. There's an overview of the building's history, which is a stunning combination of Chinese and European architectural styles, including art deco, Palladianism and a Chinese gable roof and stucco. (พิพิธภัณฑ์ภูเก็ตไทยหัว; ☎076 211224; 28 Th Krabi; admission 200B; ⏱9am-5pm)

Khao Rang
VIEWPOINT

3 Map p26, A1

For a bird's-eye view of the city, climb (or drive) up Khao Rang, 3km north-west of the town centre. A new viewing platform has opened up the commanding panoramas across Phuket Town and all the way to Chalong Bay, Laem Phanwa and Big Buddha. It's at its best during the week, when the summit is relatively peaceful. There are a few restaurants up here. It's about an hour's walk, but don't try it at night. A taxi up costs 700B. (เขารัง, Phuket Hill; P)

Phuket Heritage Trails
WALKING TOUR

4 Map p26, B2

Tap into the fascinating history of Phuket Town with these professional local guides. Discover the hidden symbolism of the Sino-Portuguese architecture, wander a variety of temples and sample Phuket foodie favourites on the Meet the Locals tour, or explore Phuket's natural beauty around Thalang District with the Off the Beaten Path itinerary. Prices include meals and transfers. Email for timings and bookings. (☎085 158 9788; www.phuketheritagetours.net; 124/1 Soi Butsaracome; tour 1500-2850B)

Chyn Pracha House
MUSEUM

5 Map p26, B3

Built in 1903 on tin-mining riches, this beautifully preserved Sino-Portuguese mansion should make any antique lover's list. The atrium foyer with its arch-framed koi pond, gorgeous Italian ceramic tiles, blue-and-white-shuttered windows and vintage

Phuket Town's Sino-Portuguese Architecture

Stroll along Th Thalang, Dibuk, Yaowarat, Ranong, Phang-Nga, Rassada and Krabi for a glimpse of Phuket Town's Sino-Portuguese architectural treasures. The most magnificent examples are the **Standard Chartered Bank** (Map p26, C3; Th Phang-Nga), Thailand's oldest foreign bank; the **THAI** (Map p26 B3; ☑076 360444; www.thaiairways. com; 78/1 Th Ranong; ⏲8am-4.30pm) office; and the old post office building, which now houses the **Phuket Philatelic Museum** (Map p26, D3; Th Montri; admission free; ⏲10am-5pm Mon-Sat). Some of the most colourfully revamped buildings line Soi Romanee, off Th Thalang.

The best-restored residential properties lie along Th Thalang, Dibuk and Krabi.

black-and-white family portraits going back generations are historical details that make visits incredibly rewarding. (Baan Chyn Pracha; ☑076 211281, 076 211167; 98 Th Krabi; admission 100B; ⏲9am-4.30pm)

Raintree Spa   SPA

6 ◉ Map p26, D2

Tucked into tranquil tropical grounds, Raintree is a step up in price, quality and atmosphere from Phuket Town's storefront spas. Skilled therapists don't just go through the motions

here. Get silky-smooth with an aloe-cucumber body wrap or indulge in a two-hour 'fruit salad' scrub (pineapple, papaya, mango). (☑081 892 1001; www.theraintreespa.com; Sino House, 1 Th Montri; massages 600-1000B; ⏲10am-9.30pm)

Blue Elephant Cooking School   COOKING COURSE

7 ◉ Map p26, B3

Master the intricate art of royal Thai cooking in a stunningly restored Sino-Portuguese mansion. Options range from half-day group lessons to private eight-dish vegetarian classes (7000B). Morning sessions visit the market. Book ahead. (☑076 354355; www.blueelephant.com; 96 Th Krabi; half-day class 3270B)

Jui Tui Shrine   TAOIST SHRINE

8 ◉ Map p26, A3

This shrine attracts those wishing to bolster their physical health through prayer. It's also the major base for serious (read: violently pierced) participants during Phuket's Vegetarian Festival (p33), which makes it a great place to stake out and snap photos like the cultural paparazzi. (Soi Puthorn; admission free; ⏲8am-8pm)

Bang Niew Shrine   TAOIST SHRINE

9 ◉ Map p26, D5

Built in 1934, this shrine honours Lao La as principal deity and is an important focus for festivities (and

Understand

Phuket's History

Phuket's history reads like an old-school Robert Louis Stevenson adventure novel. It features, among other characters, jungle-dwelling pygmies, savvy Indian and European merchants, (supposedly) marauding sea gypsies, immigrant Chinese tin miners, and cross-dressing war heroines who helped save Thailand from Burma's imperial lust.

Indian merchants founded Phuket Town in the 1st century BC. Greek geographer Ptolemy, who visited in the 3rd century AD, dubbed it 'Jang Si Lang', which later became 'Junk Ceylon', the name you'll find on ancient Thailand maps. Among Phuket's original local inhabitants were now-extinct primitive tribes similar to Malaysia's surviving Semang pygmy tribes. Meanwhile, sea nomads of Malay descent, known today as *chow lair* (sea gypsies; also spelt *chao leh*), populated the coastal areas of Phuket. They sailed from cove to cove in hardy houseboats that could weather the roughest seas, living off shellfish and turtle soup, collecting pearls and staying until each beach's resources were depleted.

In the 16th century, the first of the Europeans descended on Phuket, with Dutch, Portuguese, then French, then British traders arriving for the tin industry. By the 19th century, it was the turn of the Chinese; thousands of labourers arrived for the tin-mining boom in the latter half of the 19th century. They brought their culinary and spiritual traditions with them and, when they intermarried with local citizens, the new Baba culture was born. In the late 19th and early 20th centuries, the Baba people built up Phuket Town, constructing enormous homes blending Portuguese and Chinese styles with high ceilings and thick walls (so houses would remain cool). These impressive buildings are central Phuket Town's main attractions.

Beach lovers began arriving en masse in the 1970s, transforming Phuket into one of the world's premier beach resorts. Tourism remained strong until the devastating 2004 Boxing Day tsunami, which killed 250 people on Phuket and almost 5400 across Thailand; other estimates have it much higher. Kamala, on the west coast, was particularly badly hit. It was a dark moment in Phuket's history, but Phuketians have bounced back. Today development continues at an increasingly unsustainable rate.

brutal self-mortification) during Phuket's Vegetarian Festival (p33). (Th Ong Sim Phai; admission free; ⏱6am-6pm)

Phuket Aquarium   AQUARIUM

10 ◎ Map p26, A4

Get a glimpse of Thailand's wondrous underwater world at Phuket's popular aquarium, by the harbour on the tip of Laem Phanwa, 12km southeast of Phuket Town. There's a varied collection of tropical fish, sharks and other marine life, with helpful English-language displays. Check out the blacktip reef shark, the tiger-striped catfish resembling a marinelike zebra and the electric eel with up to 600V.

Top Tip
Phuket Taxis

Since the 2014 coup, the Thai military has cracked down on Phuket's infamously overpriced 'taxi mafia'. Meters have been introduced but, at research time, metered taxis remained tricky to find. Price boards outline *maximum* rates.

To avoid being overcharged, get the phone number of a metered taxi and use that driver throughout your stay. The best way to do this is to take a metered taxi from the airport (the easiest place to find them) upon arrival. Metered taxis are 50m to the right as you exit arrivals. Set rates are 50B for the first 2km, 12B per kilometre for the next 15km and 10B per kilometre thereafter, plus 100B 'airport tax'.

(สถานแสดงพันธุ์สัตว์น้ำภูเก็ต ☎076 391126; www.phuketaquarium.org; 51 Th Sakdidej; adult/child 180/100B; ⏱8.30am-4.30pm; P)

John Gray's Seacanoe   KAYAKING

11 ◎ Map p26, B1

The original, the most reputable and by far the most ecologically sensitive kayaking company on Phuket. The Hong by Starlight trip dodges the crowds, involves sunset paddling and will introduce you to Ao Phang-Nga's famed after-dark bioluminescence. Like any good brand in Thailand, John Gray's 'Seacanoe' name and itineraries have been frequently copied. He's 3.5km north of Phuket Town. (☎076 254505; www.johngray-seacanoe. com; 86 Soi 2/3, Th Yaowarat; adult/child from 3950/1975B)

Phuket Sealand Co   ADVENTURE SPORTS

12 ◎ Map p26, D3

This Phuket Town–based outfitter can whisk you off whitewater rafting, ziplining and ATV-riding or, if you prefer, immerse you in a nearby waterfall. Elephant rides are available, but it's worth reading up on the considerable animal welfare issues (p91) involved if you're thinking about it. (☎076 222900; www.sealandcamp.com; 125/1 Th Phang-Nga; adult/child day trip from 2300/1800B; ⏱7am-9pm)

Procession celebrating the Vegetarian Festival (p33)

Eating

Suay   INTERNATIONAL, THAI $$

Fabulous fusion at this converted house, just south of Old Town proper (see 1 ⊙ Map p26, C4) , means mouth-melting glass noodle salad, bright pomelo salad with salmon carpaccio and roasted chilli dressing, lamb-chop massaman curry, turmeric-infused sea bass wrapped in banana leaf, smoked eggplant with chilli-coconut dressing and crab meat, and an innovative *sôm·dam* (spicy green papaya salad) featuring flavour-popping mango-steen. (☏081 797 4135; www.suay restaurant.com; 50/2 Th Takua Pa; mains 15-400B; ⊙5pm-midnight)

Blue Elephant   THAI $$$

Royal Thai cuisine in royal Thai sur-rounds. Set in the beautifully restored, mustard-yellow Phra Phitak Chyn Pracha Mansion (see 7 ⊙ Map p26, B3) overlooking manicured lawns, Blue Elephant is elegant in every way, from the brass cutlery and ornately carved doors to the chequered tiled floors, stellar service and superbly prepped and presented dishes. (☏076 354355; www.blueelephant.com; 96 Th Krabi; mains 670-1000B; set menus 1350-2400B; ⊙11.30am-2.30pm & 6.30-10.30pm; ⚡☏)

Gallery Cafe

CAFE $$

13 Map p26, B3

Settle in on comfy cushions at this popular brunch cafe, surrounded by varnished-wood booths and yellow walls hung with art. The menu is full of hearty international and Thai goodies: all-day egg breakfasts, pizzas, pastas, salads, sandwiches, smoothies, homemade veggie burgers. We're still dreaming about the brilliant breakfast bagels and zingy passionfruit, lemongrass and ginger juices. (www.gallerycafe-phuket.com; 19 Th Yaowarat; mains 160-270B; ⏱8am-8pm; 📶)

The Cook

THAI, FUSION $

14 Map p26, C3

The Thai owner-chef used to cook Italian at a mega-resort, so when he opened this ludicrously inexpensive Old Town restaurant he successfully fused the two cultures. Try one of the sensational green chicken curry or *dôm yam* (spicy Thai soup) pizzas, or a classic pasta plate, and you'll see what the fuss is about. (☎076 258375; 101 Th Phang-Nga; mains 65-240B; ⏱8am-9.30pm Tue-Sun)

Chino Cafe

CAFE $$

15 Map p26, B3

A fun polished-concrete cafe with a rustic-chic feel. The tiny semi-open kitchen turns out a tasty selection of all-day breakfasts and Thai dishes, along with good coffee, a range of teas and small boxes of Phuket Town's famous cookies. (☎081 979 6190; www.facebook.com/chinocafegallery; 4 Th Thalang; mains 100-180B; ⏱8.30am-7pm; 📶)

Raya

THAI $$

16 Map p26, C2

Unrenovated, unpretentious and unbelievably good, charming Raya has been serving affordable Thai fare to Phuketians for around 20 years. This two-storey Sino-Portuguese institution keeps things authentic and old-worldly with its blue-washed wood doors, original mosaic floors, gramophone, stained glass and shuttered windows. Standout signatures include Phuketian *mŏo hong* (pepper-and-garlic-braised pork) and creamy crab-meat curry with coconut milk and rice noodles. (☎076 218155; rayarestaurant@gmail.com; 48/1 Th Dibuk; mains 180-650B; ⏱10am-10pm)

China Inn

INTERNATIONAL, THAI $$

17 Map p26, C3

The organic movement meets Phuketian cuisine at this restored turn-of-the-20th-century shophouse with beautiful detailing and carved wooden doors. It serves massaman curry with duck, spicy seafood salads, a host of veggie options, homemade yoghurt and fruit smoothies flavoured with organic honey. Opening hours can be erratic. (☎076 356239; 20 Th Thalang; dishes 150-300B; ⏱10am-7pm, to midnight Thu-Sat approx Nov-Apr, hours vary; 🍴)

Understand

Vegetarian Festival

Deafening machine-gun-like popping sounds fill the streets, the air is thick with grey-brown smoke and men and women traipse along blocked-off city roads, their cheeks pierced with skewers and knives. Some have blood streaming down their fronts or open lashes across their backs. No, this isn't a war zone, this is the **Vegetarian Festival** (www.phuketvegetarian.com; ☺late Sep-Oct), one of Phuket's most important celebrations and centred on Phuket Town. Frenzied, surreal and overwhelming barely describe it.

Local Chinese claim the festival was started in 1825 in nearby Kathu, by a theatre troupe from China who performed a nine-day penance of self-piercing, meditation and vegetarianism after becoming seriously ill for failing to propitiate the nine emperor gods of Taoism.

The festival, which takes place during the first nine days of the ninth lunar month of the Chinese calendar, celebrates the beginning of 'Taoist Lent', when devout Chinese abstain from meat, dairy and alcohol. Most obvious are the fast-paced daily processions with floats of ornately dressed children and gà·teu·i (ladyboys; also spelt kàthoey), and men and women engaged in stomach-churning self-mortification. Shop owners along Phuket Town's central streets set up altars offering nine tiny cups of tea, incense, fruit, firecrackers, candles and flowers to the nine emperor gods invoked by the festival.

Those participating as mediums bring the nine deities to earth by entering a trance state, piercing their cheeks with an impressive variety of objects, sawing their tongues or flagellating themselves with spiky metal balls. The temporarily possessed mediums (primarily men) stop at shopfront altars to pick up offerings and bless the house. Beyond the headlining gore, fabulous cheap vegetarian food stalls line the streets; many restaurants turn veg-only for the festival.

Phuket Town's festival focuses on five Chinese temples. Jui Tui Shrine (p28), off Th Ranong, is the most important, followed by Bang Niew Shrine (p28). If you stop by any procession's starting point early enough (around 6am), you may spot a surprisingly professional, latex-glove-clad crew piercing the devotees' cheeks (not for the faint-hearted).

Phuket's Tourism Authority of Thailand (p151) prints festival schedules..

Top Tip

What's On, Phuket?

The weekly English-language *Phuket Gazette* (www.phuket gazette.net) publishes information on island-wide activities, dining and entertainment, plus the latest scandals. *Phuket Wan* (www.phuketwan. com) is frequently juicier and more newsworthy. *Phuket News* (www. thephuketnews.com) is another excellent source on island life.

Eleven Two & Co

THAI, INTERNATIONAL $$

 18 Map p26, C3

This fresh energetic cafe-restaurant dishes tempting treats from classic Thai (*pàt tai*, *pá·naang* curry) to simple European (pastas, salads, burgers) and fantastic fusion, such as spicy Thai pork quesadilla, mango crepes and 'drunken seafood' pasta. Also try deliciously fresh juices; try a pineapple, watermelon, ginger and lime 'Refresher'. (www.eleventwoandco.com; 112 Th Thalang; mains 80-250B; ☺10.30am-10pm)

Brasserie

BELGIAN $$$

19 Map p26, B3

Now this is real carnivore's territory and a great spot to splurge on fine Belgian-inspired food, with serious Australian rib-eye steaks, lamb chops, spare ribs and Wagyu beef tartare with goats' cheese. Get romantic in the Provence-style courtyard or the elegant

oyster counter or crowd around the busy wooden bar with an excellent selection of Belgian beers. (☎081 970 7805; www.brasseriephuket.com; 18 Th Rassada; mains 300-500B; ☺6-11pm Wed-Mon)

Dibuk Restaurant

FUSION $$$

 20 Map p26, B2

This is more a marriage of French and Thai than actual fusion. You can have your wild boar in red-wine sauce, tortellini with lobster or steamed white snapper and searing-hot prawns steeped in lime, chilli and garlic. Considering the quality and the jazzy romantic atmosphere with chandeliers, prices are relatively reasonable. (☎076 214138; www.dibukrestaurant.com; 69 Th Dibuk; mains 240-680B; ☺11am-10.30pm)

Thanon Ranong Day Market

MARKET $

21 Map p26, B3

Phuket Town's bustling day market is all about fresh produce, tracing its history back to the days when pirates, Indians, Chinese, Malays and Europeans traded in Phuket. (Th Ranong ☺5am-noon)

Drinking

Timber Hut

CLUB

 22 Map p26, B2

Thai and expat locals have been packing out this two-floor pub-club nightly for 25 years, swilling whiskey and swaying to live bands that swing from hard rock to pure pop to hip-hop.

Viewpoint at Khao Rang (p27)

No cover charge. (☎076 211839; 118/1 Th Yaowarat; ◷6pm-2am)

Comics
BAR

23 🚇 Map p26, C3

A youthful all-Thai clientele crams into this bubbly, blue-lit, comic-covered space for mellow live music enjoyed with Thai and international beers, ciders, wines and cocktails. (www.facebook.com/Comics-Cafe-Bar-358086567609208; 44 Th Phang-Nga; ◷6pm-midnight)

Bo(ok)hemian
CAFE

24 🚇 Map p26, C3

Every town should have a coffee house this cool, with a split-level design that feels simultaneously warm and cutting-edge. Used books (for sale) line the front room, bicycles hang from the wall, and it does gourmet coffee and tea, and damn good chocolate cake. (☎098 090 0657; www.bookhemian.com; 61 Th Thalang; ◷9am-7pm Mon-Fri, to 8.30pm Sat & Sun; 🛜)

Rockin' Angels
BAR

25 🚇 Map p26, B3

This intimate colourful Old Town bar is packed with biker paraphernalia and framed LPs (the Beatles, Cindy Lauper, the Beach Boys). Weekend nights can get loud when Patrick, the Singaporean-born musician-owner, jams with his house blues band (11pm Friday; 10pm Saturday and

Sunday). Beers are cold and you'll be surrounded by a good mix of Thais and local expats. (☏089 654 9654; www.facebook.com/Rockin-Angels-Blues-Cafe-Band-245680052110080; 55 Th Yaowarat; ⏱6.30pm-1am)

Ka Jok See
CLUB

26 🍷 Map p26, C3

Dripping with Old Phuket charm this intimate century-old house has two identities: half glamorous eatery, half crazy party venue. There's good Thai food, but once the tables are cleared it becomes a bohemian madhouse party with top-notch music and – if you're lucky – some sensational extravagant

Local Life
To Market, to Market

A wonderful way to embrace Phuket Town's local flavour is by getting lost in its markets. On Sundays, Th Thalang morphs into heaving **Walking St** (Map p26 C3; Th Thalang; ⏱4-10pm Sun), where fashionable young Thais flog vintage clothing and quirky homemade goods alongside sizzling southern-Thai food carts. For something more classic, try the massive **Weekend Market** (off Th Chao Fa West; ⏱4-10pm Sat & Sun), 3km (30B by moto-taxi) southwest of town. Things are liveliest in the evening, when it's a fantastic spot for a cheap feed. Otherwise, join snacking local families for live music at **Indy Market** (Map p26 D2; Limelight Av; ⏱4-10.30pm Wed-Fri).

cabaret. Book a month or two ahead. There's no sign. (☏076 217903; kajoksee@hotmail.com; 26 Th Takua Pa; buffet per person 2500B; ⏱8pm-1am Nov-Apr, reduced hours May-Oct)

Entertainment

Suwit Muay Thai Stadium
SPECTATOR SPORT

27 ⭐ Map p26, A4

Moo·ay tai (Thai boxing; also known as *muay Thai*) bouts can be witnessed once a week at this training camp, 7km south of Phuket Town. Book at **Mark Travel & Service** (☏076 212658; woody_marktravel@hotmail.com; 1 Th Takua Pa; ⏱6am-6pm); ticket prices vary depending on where you sit. (off Rte 4021; admission general/ringside incl one-way transport 1200/1500B; ⏱fight 8.30pm Fri)

Shopping

Ranida
ANTIQUES, FASHION

28 🛍 Map p26, C3

An elegant antique gallery and boutique featuring antique Buddha statues and sculpture, organic textiles, and exquisite high-fashion clothing inspired by vintage Thai garments and fabrics. (119 Th Thalang; ⏱10.30am-7.30pm Mon-Sat)

Ban Boran Textiles
TEXTILES

Shelves at this hole-in-the-wall (see 25 🍷 Map p26, B3) are stocked high with quality silk scarves, Burmese lacquerware, sarongs, linen shirts, cute colourful bags and cotton textiles from

hiang Mai. (☎076 211563; 51 Th Yaowarat;
⏰11am-6.30pm)

rawing Room

ARTS

9 🔒 Map p26, C3

'ith a street-art vibe reminiscent of
re-boom Brooklyn, this wide-open co-
perative is by far the stand-out gallery
a town full of them. Canvasses might
e vibrant abstract squiggles or comi-
l pen-and-ink cartoons. House music
umps at low levels. (isara380@hotmail.
m; 56 Th Phang-Nga; ⏰10am-9pm)

outhwind Books

BOOKS

0 🔒 Map p26, B3

emember second-hand paperbacks?
eruse these dusty aisles for afford-
le hand-me-down titles in multiple
nguages. (☎089 724 2136; www.facebook.
m/SouthWindBooks; 3-9 Th Phang-Nga;
9am-5.30pm Mon-Sat, 10am-3pm Sun)

'ua Art Gallery & Studio

ARTS

fun and intriguing artist-owned
ophouse (see **30** 🔒 Map 26, B3) featur-
g mythical creatures and abstract
ortraits in minimalist grey-dominated
s on canvas, with splashes of vibrant
lours, crafted by a man known only
'Mr Zen'. (☎076 258208; www.wua-
tgallery.com; 1 Th Phang-Nga; ⏰9.30am-
30pm)

an Boran Antiques

ANTIQUES

1 🔒 Map p26, C3

his refined yet understated antiques
ouse holds some striking old-school

furniture, sculpture and decoration
finds (mostly Thai and Myanmarese),
along with vibrant vintage fabrics, raw
silks and silver Sri Lankan jewellery.
(☎084 683 3474; banboran.antiques@gmail.
com; 8 Th Takua Pa; ⏰10am-10pm)

Art Room Phuket

ARTS

32 🔒 Map p26, B3

Dip into a contrasting world of soothing, soft-toned Thai-life watercolours
alongside bold, powerfully, locally inspired abstract oil canvases that throw
light on hot contentious topics such
as urban expansion, sea pollution and
water shortages. (☎084 630 1582; www.
facebook.com/artbymekphat; 29 Th Yaowarat;
⏰10am-6pm)

111 Phuket Art Gallery

ARTS

33 🔒 Map p26, C3

Pick up some psychedelic art featuring local subject matter such as
Sino-Portuguese buildings covered in
overhead power lines or vivid inventive
seascapes. (www.facebook.com/111-Phuket-
Art-Gallery-593077280774171; 111 Th Phang-
Nga; ⏰9am-6pm)

Merci Beaucoup

FASHION

34 🔒 Map p26, B3

Masses of lace, sequins, frills and
adventurous patterns make for bold,
upmarket fashion choices to combine
with colour-popping jewellery, bags
and hats at this swish little women's
boutique. (Th Yaowarat; ⏰10am-6pm)

Explore

Hat Patong

If Patong were a celeb, it'd be sprawled across the covers of trashy mags daily. Its knack for turning the midlife crisis into a full-scale industry and its complete disregard for managed development make it rampant with unintentional comedy. The only thing pure here is the white sand on the beach. But if you're after a party, don't miss Patong.

The Region in a Day

Nurse that hangover with a morning dip on **Hat Patong** (p44), before soaking up the scene at **Good Luck Shrine** (p45) and indulging in a Thai herbal steam bath at **Let's Relax** (p44). Follow up with a fresh Thai lunch at **Kaab Gluay** (p47). If that sounds a little dull, devote your morning and afternoon to uncovering the Andaman's underwater wonders with **Sea Fun Divers** (p44).

Escape the buzzing jet skis and afternoon hordes by chartering a long-tail boat to more secluded **Hat Freedom** (p44). Back in Patong, throw together the perfect island-life outfit at **Baru** (p52) and **Mrs Carino** (p54), or find **Baanboonpitak** (p53) for the ultimate antiques treasure hunt.

As night rolls around, Patong kicks into action. If you haven't scored tickets for **Phuket Simon Cabaret** (p52) or *moo·ay tai* (Thai boxing; also known as *muay Thai*) at **Bangla Boxing Stadium** (p52), the bars and clubs will keep you busy. Dine at eccentric Thai-Mediterranean **Home Kitchen** (p46) before you hit the sin-city epicentre that is Th Bangla and the heaving dance floors at **Seduction** (p50) and **Illuzion** (p50).

For a local's day in Hat Patong, see p40.

Local Life

Pub & Grub Crawl Patong

Best of Hat Patong

Dining

Kaab Gluay (p47)

Baan Rim Pa (p47)

Savoey (p48)

Orchids (p48)

Places to Party

Patong Pub Crawl (p40)

Seduction (p50)

Illuzion (p50)

Sole Mio (p50)

Getting There

Taxi Private taxis to/from the airport cost 800B.

Minibus There's a shared minibus from the airport to Patong (per person 180B, minimum 10 people).

Bus A 'local bus' (actually a mini van) runs between Phuket Town's Bus Terminal 1, on Th Phang-Nga, and Patong (50B, 7am to 5pm).

Sŏrng·tăa·ou Passenger pick-up trucks run between the south end of Hat Patong and Phuket Town's Th Ranong (30B, 7am to 6pm).

Local Life
Pub & Grub Crawl Patong

A night out in Patong is obligatory for party lovers on Phuket and inevitably involves a good few laps back and forth along Th Bangla. And while bar girls playing ping pong (without paddles) may be enough to put you off your *pàt tai*, you can still have a fantastic time taking in the spectacle and hitting some bars on and around Th Bangla. This walk takes in a few of the less, er, sordid spots to fill up on beer, booze and snacks.

❶ Patong Food Park

Amble along Patong's main Th Rat Uthit, feeling your appetite grow as you check out row upon row of seafood restaurants. Near the intersection with Th Hat Patong, you'll find **Patong Food Park** (Th Rat Uthit; dishes 50-200B; ⏱4.30pm-midnight), a two-block local foodie's dream world. Forever packed with Thais and expats, it's the ideal spot to ease into a heavy night, with all kinds of fresh fish, crab

bster, roasted pork leg, steamed
hicken, satay and *sôm·đam* (spicy
reen papaya salad) carts. All cheap
nd delicious.

❷ Rock City

ollow Th Rat Uthit south and things
apidly get brighter, noisier and row-
ier. On the corner of Th Bangla and
h Rat Uthit, and impossible to miss,
s your next drinking spot, **Rock City**
www.rockcityphuket.com; 169 Th Rat Uthit;
8pm-2am). This dark den of rock
ives on the glory of AC/DC, Metallica
nd Guns N' Roses tribute bands,
which attract a headbanging crowd
f tourists and locals from 9.45pm
nwards. A taster for Th Bangla.

❸ Thanon Bangla

or many travellers, Th Bangla *is*
Patong: go-go bars, ping-pong shows
nd dusk-until-dawn debauchery. For
others, it's a one-night experience before a hasty retreat to their beachside
resort. Th Bangla is beer and bar-girl
central, featuring spectacular go-go
extravaganzas with the usual mix of
bored-looking gyrating Thai girls and
usually red-faced Western men. But,
on the surface, the atmosphere is
more carnival than carnage, and you'll
meet plenty of peers pushing through
the crowds to the bar.

❹ Aussie Bar

We've all seen Aussie-themed bars, but
Patong's **Aussie Bar** (www.aussiebar
phuket.com; Th Bangla; ⏰9.30am-2.30am;

⏸) is pretty good fun if you've had
enough of Bangla's street circus. You
might be on holiday but there's no
need to miss the football, rugby, ten-
nis, cricket etc when you've got huge
sports screens splashing it across from
every angle. Get competitive on the
pool tables or foosball.

❺ Molly Malone's

Standing strong since 1999, **Molly
Malone's** (☎076 292771; www.molly
malonesphuket.com; 94 Th Thawiwong;
⏰10am-2am) flaunts itself as Phuket's
oldest pub. Hidden within a classic
green-and-gold Irish pub facade, it's
warm, laid-back and crammed full of
dark-wood furniture, sports screens
and pool tables. Live music kicks
off around 10pm. If you fancy, order
away on burgers, baguettes and jacket
potatoes.

❻ Lucky 13

Head back east to modern-minimalist
expat fave **Lucky 13** (☎091 824 0013;
www.facebook.com/Lucky-13-Sandwich-
Patong-664452587010019; 184/16 Th
Pangmuang Sai Kor; dishes 50-290B;
⏰24hr; ⏸🍴). With flavour-packed
sandwiches, outrageously popular
burgers and nonstop service, it's the
perfect final pit stop. Pick your bread
(baguette, ciabatta, focaccia) and
layer on fillings. Smoked salmon with
wasabi? Steak sandwich? Veg-friendly
aubergine and hummus? Now you can
hit the clubs – but we take no respon-
sibility for you from here on!

Th Phra Barami

12 ⊗

4029

Wat Suwan
Khiri Wong
(500m)

33 30 ⊕⊕

Th Phra Barami

5 ⊙ Nicky's
Handlebar

Th Sai Nam Yen

Bmuang Sai Kor

Good
Luck
6 ⊙ Shrine

34 ⊕

13 ⊗

35 ⊕

25 ⊕

Th Phra
Barami

Th Chaloem Phra Kiat

19 ⊗

Th Rat Uthit

Th Paradise

22

Th Hat Patong

36 ⊕

Royal
Paradise
Complex

11 ⊗
14 ⊗

Th Thawiwong

Hat 3 ⊙
Patong

Th Sawatdirak

Th Thawiwong

31

Hat ⊕
Patong

16 ⊗

8 ⊗
Swasana ⊙
Spa

17 ⊕

Ao Patong

ANDAMAN
SEA

For reviews see
⊙	Experiences	p44
⊗	Eating	p46
⊕	Drinking	p50
⊕	Entertainment	p52
⊕	Shopping	p52

400 m
0.2 miles

0
0

Ⓝ

Th Nanai

Relax 4

23

en Sabal

32

Spa 9

Soi Post Pum Thai
Office Cooking
7 School
15
Soi Prisanee

Th Thawi

Soi 1

24

18

Soi Kepsap

Th Ruamchai

Th Sirirach

Soi
Permpong
Pattana

29

26
2 1

Sŏrng·tǎa·ou
to Phuket
Town

Th Prachanukro

Sea Bees
10

Experiences

Hat Freedom
BEACH

1 Map p42, C8

If Patong is suffocating you, escape to a whole different world on this pristine slice of golden sand. It's just 15 minutes or a 1500B (return) long-tail ride south around the headland from Hat Patong. You can also get here via a challenging cliff walk from a car park 800m beyond Avista Hideaway Resort, past the southern end of Hat Patong.

> ☑ Top Tip
>
> **Tiger Kingdom**
>
> During your stay, you'll inevitably be handed a brochure flaunting Phuket's controversial Tiger Kingdom. Launched in 2013, Tiger Kingdom Phuket offers hundreds of daily visitors the chance to stroke, feed and pose for selfies with 'domesticated' tigers (cubs and full-grown adults).
>
> As with Thailand's other tiger-centric attractions, worries of animal welfare and human safety abound. There are constant reports about tigers allegedly being mal-treated, confined to small cages and sedated to keep them docile. Tiger Kingdom denies these allegations. In 2014 an Australian tourist was seriously mauled at Tiger Kingdom. The tiger in question was 'retired'.
>
> Given the significant animal welfare issues involved, Lonely Planet does not recommend visiting Tiger Kingdom.

Sea Fun Divers
DIVING

2 Map p42, C8

An outstanding, very professional diving operation, with high standards, impeccable service and keen, knowledgeable instructors. It's based at Le Meridien resort at the southern end of Patong. (☑076 340480; www. seafundivers.com; 29 Soi Karon Nui; 2/3 dives 4100/4500B, Open Water certification 18,400B; ⊙9am-6pm)

Hat Patong
BEACH

3 Map p42, D3

It may not be a blissful stretch of untouched paradise, but Patong's ever-popular broad white-sand beach is action-packed with loads of water activities on offer – and you don't have to venture far for after-dark fun.

Let's Relax
SPA

4 Map p42, E5

The hushed atrium, infused with eucalyptus, is the perfect place to mull over your relaxation strategy. Will it be foot reflexology then a floral body scrub? A Thai herbal steam bath before a hot-stone massage and a facial? The all-in Phuket Day Dream package (4000B)? Life is full of tough decisions. Online or walk-in bookings only. (☑076 366724; www. letsrelaxspa.com; 184/14 Th Pangmuang Sai

Hat Freedom

Kor; massage/treatment from 300/1200B; ⏱10am-midnight)

Nicky's Handlebar ADVENTURE TOUR

5 Map p42, E2

The custom-made big-beast bikes are just begging to be taken for a spin, but they aren't for amateurs. Nicky has been leading Harley tours around Phuket for over a decade. Full-day itineraries tour Phang-Nga Province and there are half-day options, plus Harley rentals for independent explorations (from 4800B). You'll need a big-bike license from home. Hit the bar (p50) for post-drive refreshments.

(☎076 343211; www.nickyhandlebars.com; 41 Th Rat Uthit; half-/full-day tour incl bike hire from 7000/9000B)

Good Luck Shrine SHRINE

6 Map p42, D1

A beautiful, golden Bodhisattva statue, adorned with rainbow-coloured ribbons and guarded by carved elephants festooned with flowers, incense and candles. Given the sea backdrop, this is a pleasant spot to connect with the divine or simply make a wish and savour the sound of...traffic. (cnr Th Tawiwong & Th Phra Barami)

Pum Thai Cooking School

COOKING COURSE

7 ⊙ Map p42, D5

This restaurant–cookery school (with branches in Thailand, France and the UK) holds several daily one-dish (30 minutes) to six-hour classes. Popular, four-hour 'Little Wok' classes include a market tour and a take-home cookbook. (☑076 346269; www.pumthai foodchain.com; 204/32 Th Rat Uthit; class 500-7500B)

Swasana Spa

SPA

8 ⊙ Map p42, D3

This professional four-star spa is right on the beach at the quiet(ish) northern end of Hat Patong. The best deal is the traditional Thai massage (1100B), though it often has good discounts. You'll be nestled in a cool glass cube on a cushy floor mat with ocean views. (☑076 340138; www.impiana.

◯ Local Life

Wat Suwan Khiri Wong

This slightly overgrown yet peaceful **temple complex** (Wat Patong; cnr Th Phra Barami & Th Phisit Karani; admission free; ⊙dawn-dusk), just off Th Phra Barami at the northeast end of town, is a welcome respite from Patong's chaos. Unlike Phuket's more tourist-friendly temples, it's home to rambling roosters, dozing dogs and (usually) locked temple doors. The crematorium's elaborately tiered roof is beautiful.

com; 41 Th Thawiwong; massage 1100-1900B; ⊙10am-9pm)

Sovrana Spa

SPA

9 ⊙ Map p42, D5

Part salon, part shop full of all-natural oils, soaps and creams, Sovrana is a popular day-spa choice with reasonable prices and a variety of treatments. Indulge in a coconut-oil massage, a white-orchid facial or, if you've notched up too much beach time, an aloe after-sun facial, all using in-house products. It's just back from Th Rat Uthit, opposite Jung Ceylon. (☑081 683 1741; www.sovranaspa.com; 198/13 Th Rat Uthit; massage 300-700B; ⊙10am-midnight)

Sea Bees

DIVING

10 ⊙ Map p42, A6

An excellent, efficient, German-managed diving school offering fun dives to Ko Phi-Phi and King Cruiser Wreck, Open Water certification (15,000B) and Similan Islands live-aboards (from 18,900B). Branches across Phuket. (☑076 292969; www. sea-bees.com; Amari Coral Beach Resort, Hat Patong; 2 dives 3750B; ⊙9am-6pm)

Eating

Home Kitchen

INTERNATIONAL $$$

11 ✕ Map p42, D1

White leather, faded tables, floaty fabrics, burning lanterns and neon lighting crash together with

Mediterranean flair. This crazily beautiful, quirky-chic dining room/cocktail bar shaped like a ship's hull is a stunning work of art. And the creative Thai-Mediterranean food is fab too. Try avocado and crabmeat salad, squid-ink pasta with salmon, massaman Wagyu beef, deep-fried *pá-naang*-curry sea bass and perfectly crispy Parmesan-coated chips. (📞093 764 6753; www.facebook.com/HOME.kitchen.bar.bed; 314 Th Phra Barami, Hat Kalim; mains 300-800B; 🕐5am-1am; 🛜)

Kaab Gluay   THAI $

12 🍴 Map p42, E1

It's hardly Patong's most peaceful spot, but this easygoing roadside eatery is a hit for its authentic, affordable Thai food, with switched-on staff and well-spelt (!) menus to match. Unpretentious dining happens under a huge tin roof. Expect red-curry prawns, chicken satay, sweet-and-sour fish, deep-fried honeyed chicken, classic noodles and stir-fries, and 30-plus takes on spicy Thai salads. (📞076 346832; 58/3 Th Phra Barami; dishes 60-165B; 🕐11am-2am; 🛜)

Chicken Rice Briley   THAI $

13 🍴 Map p42, E3

One of few diners in Patong Food Park to offer sustenance while the sun shines. Steamed chicken breast is served on a bed of rice with a bowl of chicken broth with crumbled bits of meat; dip it in the fantastic chilli sauce.It does a popular stewed pork on rice, plus mango with sticky rice.

Top Tip

Jet Ski Scams

Although the Phuket governor declared jet skis illegal in 1997 and they were (theoretically) re-banned in 2014, ban enforcement is another issue. If you're hiring a jet ski, especially on Hat Patong, be aware of one of Phuket's most well-publicised scams. There are endless reports of unscrupulous jet ski owners who, upon your return, claim you've caused damage to the watercraft that was, in fact, pre-existing. Things can turn nasty: tourists constantly report extortion attempts, physical threats and intervention by police, often allegedly involved in the scam. To avoid these unpleasant encounters, insist on inspecting the jet ski prior to use, particularly underneath and along the sides. Take photos.

There's a reason it's perennially packed. (📞081 597 8380; Patong Food Park, Th Rat Uthit; meals 50-60B; 🕐6am-9pm)

Baan Rim Pa   THAI $$$

14 🍴 Map p42, D1

Refined Thai fare is served with a side order of spectacular views at this institution. Standards are high, with prices to match, but romance is in the air, with candlelight and piano music aplenty. Book ahead, button up and tuck in. (📞076 340789; www.baanrimpa.com; 223 Th Phra Barami; mains 290-750B; 🕐noon-10pm)

La Gritta

ITALIAN $$$

10 Map p42, A6

A spectacularly positioned (see 10 Map p42, A6), modern Italian restaurant serving up huge portions of deliciously creamy pastas and gourmet pizzas. With comfy booths, gorgeous beach views and a deck just centimetres above the boulder-strewn shore at the south end of Hat Patong, there are few better settings for a sunset Chalong Bay Rum mojito (p93). (076 292697; www.lagritta.com; Amari Coral Beach Resort, Hat Patong; mains 400-800B; 10am-midnight;)

Ella

INTERNATIONAL $$

15 Map p42, C5

A moulded-concrete, industrial-feel bistro-cafe that's a lovely surprise. Inventive all-day breakfasts feature spicy Rajasthani scrambled eggs, massaman chicken tacos, omelettes stuffed with chicken and veg, and baguette French toast with caramelised banana. (076 344253; www.facebook.com/EllaBistro; 100/19-20 Soi Post Office; mains 200-400B; 9am-11pm;)

Top Tip

Hat, Beach...Same, Same

If your Thai is a little rusty, the most important word you'll probably need to know on Phuket is 'Hat'(*hàht*). 'Hat' means 'beach' and you'll notice places are referred to as Patong Beach or Hat Patong, Kata Beach or Hat Kata...Same, same. Also, 'Ko' (*gò*) means island.

The Beach

THAI, SEAFOOD $$

16 Map p42, D3

If you fancy decent Thai food and a string of predictable, reliable seafood choices by the beach, wander over to this long-running shack. It's slightly overpriced, but the setting is fantastic. (076 345944; 49 Th Thawiwong; mains 180-350B; 8am-11.30pm)

Savoey

THAI $$

17 Map p42, D4

On an island packed with weighed-to-order fish grills, Savoey is an astoundingly popular choice. Its huge streetside ice shelf is packed with lobsters, prawns, grouper, red snapper, sole, sea bass and barracuda. There's one menu across a mix of indoor-outdoor dining rooms. Dishes, including non-seafood Thai faves, are tasty and prices pretty reasonable. (076 341171; 136 Th Thawiwong; mains 250-490B; 6.30am-midnight)

The Orchids

THAI $

18 Map p42, C5

Get your fantastic, cheap Thai food in a homey, friendly setting with attentive staff. The *larb gai* (minced chicken salad mixed with chili, mint and coriander) is delicious, and the Orchids serves up all your favourite noodle, rice, soup and curry classics, including *đôm yam gûng* (intensely spicy prawn soup). Eat in or take

Baan Rim Pa restaurant (p47)

away. (📞076 340462; www.theorchid
spatongbeach.com; 78/3-4 Soi Permpong Pattana; mains 85-320B; 🕙11am-11pm)

Sandwich Shoppe   CAFE $

19 🍴 Map p42, D3

You're the master of your meal at
this smart, quiet, tucked-away cafe.
Build your own sandwiches, salads,
bagels and breakfasts from an array of
options covering everything from the
bread to the dressing. If you can't decide, there are loads of premade good-
ies, including flaky pastries, chunky
French toast, mushroom omelettes
and smoked-salmon muffins. (📞076

290468; 26-27 Th Aroonsom Plaza; dishes
100-180B; 🕙8am-6pm; 🛜)

Sala Bua   FUSION $$$

Enjoy award-winning fusion cuisine
with an Asian-Mediterranean vibe in a
classy seaside four-star resort setting
(see 8 👁 Map p42, D3). Start with smoked
salmon Caesar salad or rock lobster,
avocado and roasted veg salad, then
move on to wood-fired pizzas, seafood-
packed spaghetti or *pá·naang* curry
osso buco. (📞076 340138; www.impiana.
com; 41 Th Thawiwong; mains 300-1900B;
🕙11am-11pm)

Drinking

Seduction
CLUB

20 Map p42, D5

International DJs, professional-grade sound system and forever the best dance party on Phuket, without question. (www.facebook.com/seductiondisco; 70/3 Th Bangla; ⏰10pm-5am)

Illuzion
CLUB

21 Map p42, D4

Patong's hottest new mega-club is a sparkly multi-level mishmash of dance and gymnastics shows, international DJs, regular ladies' nights, all-night electronic beats, and more bars than you could ever count. (www.illuzion phuket.com; 31 Th Bangla; ⏰10pm-6am)

Sole Mio
BAR

A whimsically decorated bar with a Caribbean-feel, crafted using recycled corrugated tin, strings of shells and reclaimed pastel-washed wood. It's right by the beach (see 16 Map p42, D3), pulses with pop songs and is fuelled by middling cocktails and Chang draught. There are worse ways to spend an afternoon. (📞081 5378116; Th Thawiwong; ⏰10am-midnight; 📶)

Boat Bar
GAY, BAR

22 Map p42, E4

Phuket's original gay nightspot, and still its only dance club, gets busy with a lively, mostly gay crowd. Don't miss the midnight and 2am cabarets. (📞076 341237; www.facebook.com/Boat bar; 125/20 Royal Paradise Hotel Complex; ⏰9pm-4pm)

Nicky's Handlebar
BAR

This fun biker bar (see 5 Map p42, E2) welcomes all, wheels or no wheels. Once a bit of a dive, Nicky's has never looked better. Ashtrays crafted from bike parts rest on the metal bar and weighty menus are made from hub-caps and heavy disk brakes. You can get your own wheels here by asking about Harley tours and hire (from 4800B). (📞076 343211; www.nickyhandle bars.com; 41 Th Rat Uthit ; ⏰7.30am-1am; 📶)

Understand
Connect Four!

Is it an innocent children's game or a bar girl's ruse to score your cash 100B at a time? You'll find out on Th Bangla. Connect Four seems an innocent enough pastime when you stroll into the bar. You'll play a game or two for a few hundred baht while you sip a few Singhas. But here's the catch: your opponent is a Connect Four mastermind. She will win, quickly and easily. You'll go for double or nothing. Your friends will help you strategise. And she'll win again. Even easier this time. And every time after that. Be afraid. Be very afraid.

Understand

Sex Tourism

--- --- --- --- --- --- --- --- --- --- --- --- ---

Thailand has a long and complex relationship with prostitution. Today it's an industry that most obviously targets foreign tourists – a legacy left behind from the Vietnam War days. Despite the military government's crackdown on corruption in 2014 and 2015 (which included fining and arresting sex workers in Pattaya), sex tourism is very visible on Phuket, particularly in Patong.

Due to international pressure from the UN, prostitution was declared illegal in 1960. Unfortunately, laws against prostitution are often ambiguous, unenforced and, according to sex-worker organisation EMPOWER (Education Means Protection Of Women Engaged in Recreation), outdated. Furthermore, the unintended consequence of prostitution prohibitions is the lawless working environment it creates for men and women who enter the industry. Sex work becomes the domain of criminal networks that are often involved in other illicit activities, circumventing laws through bribes, intimidation and violence.

Sex workers are not afforded the rights of other workers. There is no minimum wage; no required vacation, sick leave or break time; no deductions for social security or employee-sponsored health insurance; and no legal redress. Bars set their own punitive rules that fine workers if they don't smile enough, arrive late, gain weight or don't meet the drink quota. EMPOWER reported that many sex workers owe money to the bar at the end of the month through these deductions. In effect, they're paying to be prostitutes.

According to ECPAT (End Child Prostitution & Trafficking), in 2011 there were up to 60,000 children involved in prostitution in Thailand, though estimates are unreliable and vary wildly. In 1996 Thailand passed a reform law to address the issue of child prostitution (defined into two tiers: 15 to 18 years old and under 15). Fines and jail time are assigned to customers, establishment owners and even parents involved in child prostitution (under the old law only prostitutes were culpable). Many countries have extraterritorial legislation that allows nationals to be prosecuted in their own country for such crimes committed in Thailand. Responsible travellers can help to stop child-sex tourism by reporting suspicious behaviour on dedicated hotlines (☎1300 or ☎1191) or reporting the offender directly to the relevant embassy.

Chicco Juice

JUICE BAR

23 Map p42, E5

If Patong's pace has drained the life out of you, refuel with some healthy tropical goodness as this podlike juice stall. Try a signature Vitamax C juice packed with orange, apple and passionfruit, or a creamy wild mango yoghurt smoothie, and you'll be ready for the next round in no time. (www.facebook.com/chiccophuket; Jung Ceylon, off Th Pangmuang Sai Kor; ◷10am-10pm)

Craft Beer Lounge

BAR

24 Map p42, D6

Tapping into one of the world's latest booze crazes, this sleekly contemporary boutique beer bar stocks over 100 international draught and craft labels, plus local brands. Sink into a cosy rattan lounge chair or tackle the pool table amid soft neon lighting and background house beats. It's tucked into the back of the Grand Mercure's lobby. (www.grandmercurephuketpatong.com; Grand Mercure Phuket Patong, Soi 1, Th Rat Uthit; ◷10am-11.30pm)

Zag Club

GAY, BAR

25 Map p42, E4

Packed-out gay-scene favourite Zag Club hosts shimmering cabarets at 10.30pm, 11.30pm, midnight and 2am. In between, everyone drinks and dances to booming chart-toppers. (123/8-9 Royal Paradise Complex; ◷8pm-4.30am)

Entertainment

Phuket Simon Cabaret

CABARET

26 Map p42, C8

About 500m south of town, Simon puts on fun, colourful trans cabarets. The 600-seat theatre is grand, the costumes are glittery, feathery extravaganzas and the ladyboys are convincing. It's noticeably geared towards an Asian audience and the house is usually full – book ahead. (☏076 342114; www.phuket-simoncabaret.com; 8 Th Sirirach; adult 700-800B, child 500-600B; ◷shows 6pm, 7.45pm & 9.30pm)

Bangla Boxing Stadium

SPECTATOR SPORT

27 Map p42, E5

Old name, same game: a packed line-up of competitive *moo-ay tai* bouts featuring Thai and foreign fighters. (☏076 273416; www.banglaboxingstadium patong.com; Th Pangmuang Sai Kor; admission 1700-2500B; ◷9pm Wed, Fri & Sun)

Shopping

Baru

FASHION

28 Map p42, D4

Packed in a hurry and managed to misplace your bikini? Relax, Baru has your back, with stacks of hot, skimpy and well-priced candy-coloured bikinis to choose from. Light wraps, floaty kaftans and beach-chic dresses in subtle tribal patterns leave slightly

Phuket Simon Cabaret

more to the imagination and hit that smart-casual island evening vibe perfectly. Young, fresh and fun. (☏076 343536; www.barufashion.com; Kee Plaza; ☺11.30am-10.30pm)

Baanboonpitak ANTIQUES. CRAFTS

 29 Map p42, C7

Hidden in this dusty, easy-to-miss antiques room, at the southern end of Patong, is an array of teak sculpture, delicate paintings, some excellent bronze work, massive buffalo-skin drums, bejewelled royal dogs, wood-carved elephants and a lot of high-quality teak furniture. Dig around and you're bound to find something beautiful. The shopkeeper can arrange shipping. (☏081 569 6474; baanboonpitak phuket@hotmail.com; 30 Th Prachanukhro; ☺10am-7pm)

The Nop Art ARTS

30 Map p42, E1

Around the Th Rat Uthit and Th Phra Barami intersection, at the north end of Patong, sits a cluster of small art galleries worth a browse if you're looking for some original local artwork. This is the standout for its bright, bold canvases, both abstract and of classic Thai scenes: floating markets, coconut drinks, tigers, elephants and boats bobbing on the sea. (☏089 197 6778; www.facebook.com/thenopart; 133 Th Phra Barami; ☺9am-10pm)

Mrs Carino   FASHION

31 🔒 Map p42, D4

Throw together your beach-glitz wardrobe at this tiny colour-packed haven of breezy Bali-made dresses, flowery prints, flimsy tops and summery shoes. (Kee Plaza; ⊙11am-11pm)

Jung Ceylon   SHOPPING CENTRE

32 🔒 Map p42, D5

Now this is a cool, gleaming shopping centre that's a pleasure to kill time in. The major multinationals (Apple, Starbucks, MNG, Adidas) are well represented here, as are plush cinemas and small-scale massage parlours, and the Phuket Town–inspired Sino-Phuket wing has a decent international restaurant row. Outside, surrounded by pools and musical fountains (yes, really), stands a life-size model of a Chinese junk ship. (www.jungceylon.com; Th Rat Uthit; ⊙11am-10pm)

Art Heart Gallery   ARTS

33 🔒 Map p42, E1

Vibrant abstract artworks make Art Heart a highlight among the collection of local-artist galleries on this corner. (📱087 621 5344; cnr Th Rat Uthit & Th Phra Barami; ⊙9am-5pm Mon-Sat)

Bookshop   BOOKS

34 🔒 Map p42, E3

A low-key secondhand stall stocking paperbacks in a variety of languages

Understand
LGBT Phuket

Although Bangkok and Pattaya host big gay pride celebrations, the **Phuket Gay Pride Festival** (www.phuket-pride.org; ⊙usually Apr) is widely considered the best in Thailand, possibly even Southeast Asia. Though the date has changed several times since the festival's inception in 1999, it usually lands in April. Whenever it blooms, (mostly male) revellers from all over the world flock to the island – to Patong, specifically. The four-day weekend party takes in a beach volleyball tournament, cruises to nearby islands, beauty contests and, of course, the Grand Parade, during which floats, cheering crowds and beautiful sparkly costumes take over Patong's streets. In recent years, the festival has included fundraising and social-responsibility campaigns to increase awareness of child prostitution, substance abuse and HIV.

At any other time, you'll find Phuket's gay pulse in the network of streets that link Patong's Royal Paradise Hotel with Th Rat Uthit. It's a predominantly male scene. Popular hang-outs include Boat Bar (p50) and Zag Club (p52).

For updates on future festivals and the local gay scene, check out **Gay Patong** (www.gaypatong.com).

Jung Ceylon

ranging from German, Scandinavian languages and English to Japanese. (Th Rat Uthit; ⊙10am-10pm)

Tawan Gallery ARTS

35 🔒 Map p42, E3

Peruse the lively works of five local artists and see them in action within this laid-back gallery crammed full of colourful cartoon-like canvases of elephants, serious semi-abstract portraits and the odd Thai landscape.

(☎076 296113; tawun2003@hotmail.com; 97/1 Th Rat Uthit; ⊙11am-11pm)

Metal Art ARTS

36 🔒 Map p42, E4

Sci-fi robotic sculptures, motorcycles and homewares crafted entirely from scrap-metal car parts crowd this quirky art shop. You've got everything from the *Terminator* to Ned Kelly – and the kids love it. (☎089 470 6455; metalartphuket@yahoo.com; Th Rat Uthit; ⊙10am-10pm)

Explore

Hat Karon & Hat Kata

Embodying all that's wonderful about Phuket, the conjoined twin beach towns of Kata and Karon are deservedly popular destinations. Kata is an energetic blend of bohemia and ritz. Karon is the chilled-out, scruffier, *slightly* seedier older sibling. Their long beaches, great eateries, host of activities and many bars – minus Patong's excesses – reel in families, backpackers and visitors from all walks of life.

The Region in a Day

Stretch straight into the day with a 9am body-bending session at **Kata Hot Yoga** (p60). Then laze in beachside luxury at **Re Ká Ta Beach Club** (p62) or get pummelled into shape at **Spa Royale** (p62), **Baray Spa** (p60) or **The Spa** (p62), depending on where you're based. Grab lunch on the cheap at **Pad Thai Shop** (p64) or **Kata Mama** (p64).

From here, take your pick between a lazy beach-bliss afternoon at **Hat Kata Yai** (p60) or **Hat Karon** (p60), an exhilarating surf session with **Phuket Surf** (p62) or a round of minigolf at wacky kids' favourite **Dino Park** (p63). If you love Phuket's style, swing by **Baru** (p68) and **Siam Handicraft** (p69) for breezy beach outfits.

Hike up to **After Beach Bar** (p67) for a sublime sunset with panoramic views and Bob Marley beats, and grab a beer and *pàt tai* while you're here. Otherwise go all out with a swanky Thai-Mediterranean dinner at **Boathouse Wine & Grill** (p64), before heading to **Ska Bar** (p66) or **Surf House** (p62) to drink the night away.

 Best of Hat Karon & Hat Kata

Dining

Boathouse Wine & Grill (p64)

Pad Thai Shop (p64)

Mom Tri's Kitchen (p64)

Places to Party

Ska Bar (p66)

After Beach Bar (p67)

Mr Pan's Art Space (p67)

Getting There

Taxi Taxis between the airport and Karon/Kata cost 1000/1200B. From Phuket Town is 600B; between Kata and Karon is 200B to 300B.

Minibus Minibuses run from the airport to Karon and Kata (per person 200B; minimum 10 people).

Sŏrng·tǎa·ou These passenger pick-up trucks run from Phuket Town's Th Ranong to Hat Kata, stopping on Th Pak Bang, and Hat Karon (30B, 7.30am to 6pm).

Wat
Karon

KARON

The Spa

Th Patak East

Th Vitad

29
23
11
24

Th Karon (Patak West)

Hat 4
Karon

Hat
Karon

Th Karon
(Patak West)

Sŏrng·tăa·ou
& Taxi Stop

Th Luang
Phor Chuan

Th Patak East

Sunrise 7
Divers

20

Karon
Plaza

17

Th Thai Na

4028

Amazing
Bike Tours

6

21
32
22

Dive
Asia

16

31

Dino
Park 14

19

Aspasia

13

Th Laem Sai

Ao Karon

ANDAMAN SEA

Big Buddha (10.5km)

Kumbiensii

Th Patak East

⊙27 Th Kade Kwan

Adventure

⊙5

Baray Spa

12⊙

30⊙

KATA

⊗18

Sŏrng·tǎa·ou & Taxi Stop

Th Koktanod (Patak West)

⊗28 Kata Hot Yoga

Kata (Patak West)

Surf House

⊙

1

2

Th Koktanod

4233 Th Kata-Sai Yuan

Th Pak Bang

3⊙

8⊙ ⊗

10⊙ 25

Phuket Surf

Th Koktanod

Hat Kata Yai

Hat Kata Yai

Boathouse Cooking Class

Re Ká Ta Beach Club

15

Infinite Luxury Spa

26⊙

Th Kata Noi

Spa 9⊙ Royale

Hat Kata Noi

Hat Kata Yai

Ao Kata Yai

Ao Kata Noi

Laem Sai

Ko Pu

For reviews see	
⊙ Experiences	p60
⊗ Eating	p64
⊗ Drinking	p66
⊗ Shopping	p68

0 ——— 1 km
0 ——— 0.5 miles

◁⊙N

Experiences

Boathouse Cooking Class
COOKING COURSE

1 Map p58, D6

Kata's top fine-dining restaurant offers fantastic Thai cooking classes with its renowned chef. (☏076 330015; www.boathousephuket.com; 182 Th Koktanod, Hat Kata; 1-/2-day class 2570/4095B; ☉class 10am Wed, Sat & Sun)

Kata Hot Yoga
YOGA

2 Map p58, D6

Craving more heat? At Kata Hot Yoga, Bikram's famous asana series is taught over 90 minutes in a sweltering room by the expert owner and an international roster of visiting instructors. All levels welcome; no bookings needed. Multi-class packages offer good deals. (☏076 605950; www.katahotyoga.com; 217 Th Koktanod, Hat Kata; per class 550B; ☉classes 9am, 5.15pm & 7.15pm Mon-Fri, 9am & 5.15pm Sat & Sun)

Hat Kata Yai
BEACH

3 Map p58, C5

Hat Kata is carved in two by a jutting headland. Hat Kata Yai (known as the main Kata beach) lies on the north side, while **Hat Kata Noi** unfurls to the south. Both are stunning beaches that retain their village bohemian feel despite some upmarket dining and resorts.

Hat Karon
BEACH

4 Map p58, C1

This long stretch of squeaky-fine sand is popular with families and, while it does get busy, there's always plenty of space to spread out. During the April-October low season, you can take surf lessons (one hour 1200B) and rent surfboards/bodyboards (per hour 250/100B) at its south end.

Baray Spa
SPA

5 Map p58, D5

Hidden away in a lush tropical garden full of interwoven canals and gushing waterfalls, this is a quality spa with a sophisticated edge. Keep classic with a traditional Thai massage or spice things up with a full-body coffee scrub or a seaweed bust-firming treatment.

Local Life
Wat Karon

Set back from the road in northern Karon is the relatively new, impeccably maintained **Wat Karon** (Map p58, C1; Th Patak East, Hat Karon; admission free; ☉dawn-dusk), with a small shrine occupied by a seated black-stone Buddha. Behind stands the striking tiered-roof crematorium, which opens only on ceremonial days. The grounds are lush with banana, palm and mango trees. It's particularly popular for its Tuesday and Saturday night market (from 5pm) full of clothes, accessories and food stalls.

Dragon statue, Hat Karon

Sawasdee Village, 38 Th Kade Kwan, Hat Kata; massage 1300-2600B; ⏰10am-10pm)

Amazing Bike Tours CYCLING

6 Map p58, D4

This highly popular Kata-based adventure outfitter leads small groups on half-day bicycle tours through Khao Phra Thaew Royal Wildlife & Forest Reserve. It also runs terrific day trips around Ko Yao Noi. Prices include bikes, helmets, meals, water and national park entry fees. (✆087 263 2031; www.amazingbiketoursthailand.asia; 191 Th Patak East, Hat Kata; day trip adult/child 2900/2500B)

Sunrise Divers DIVING

7 Map p58, C3

Managed by a long-time Phuket blogger, Phuket's biggest live-aboard agent organises a range of budget to luxury multi-day dives to the Similan and Surin Islands, Myanmar's Mergui Archipelago and Ko Phi-Phi. Also arranges day-trip dives, including to Ko Phi-Phi and the Similans. (✆084 626 4646, 076 398040; www.sunrise-divers.com; 269/24 Th Patak East, Hat Karon; 2/3 dives 3200/3800B, live-aboards from 12,900B; ⏰9am-5pm)

Re Ká Ta Beach Club

BEACH CLUB

8 Map p58, D6

Of Phuket's (controversially) popular beach clubs, gleaming-white Re Ká Ta is one of the chicest. It's part of the Boathouse family. Entry bags you a day of glamour, lounging on faux-leather beds or sipping passionfruit mojitos in the beachfront infinity pool surrounded by colour-changing lamps – and goes towards drinks and food (mains 300B to 1000B). Wednesdays mean free admission and manicures for girls. (076 330421; www.rekata phuket.com; 184 Th Koktanod, Hat Kata; day pass 1500B)

Spa Royale

SPA

9 Map p58, C7

With organic spa products, trickling water features, seaside treatment

---

Top Tip

Surf House

If you've got kids in tow, don't miss **Surf House** (Map p58, D6; 081 979 7737; www.surfhousephuket.com; 4 Mu 2, Th Pak Bang, Hat Kata; 9.30am-11.30pm;). This bar-entertainment spot across the street from Hat Kata Yai serves both beer and artificial waves. Kids will love the sloped surf slide on which riders show off wakeboarding skills for as long as they can stay upright. Everyone else can kick back in the bar over icy Changs and watch the show.

---

rooms and highly skilled therapists, this is one of the finest spas in southern Phuket. The soothing 90-minute cucumber wrap is a godsend if you've notched up a few too many hours under the sun. (076 333568; www.villa royalephuket.com; 12 Th Kata Noi, Hat Kata Noi; massage from 3200B; 10am-7pm)

Phuket Surf

SURFING

10 Map p58, C6

Offers private 1½-hour surf lessons plus board rentals. Check the website for info on local surf breaks. (087 889 7308; www.phuketsurfing.com; Hat Kata Yai; lesson 1500B, board rental per hour/day 150/500B; 8am-7pm Apr-late Oct)

The Spa

SPA

11 Map p58, C1

Rooms trail off a tree-filled tropical garden and bowls of flower petals lie strewn around: this is one of Karon's most ambient spas. Your mind will be revitalised, your body scrubbed with green tea or red wine, and your skin given a glow with Dead Sea salts, before you're dunked in an aromatic floral milk bath. (076 396139; www. movenpick.com; Mövenpick Resort, 509 Th Karon/Patak West, Hat Karon; massage from 1700B; 10am-10pm)

Rumblefish Adventure

DIVING

12 Map p58, D5

A terrific boutique dive shop offering all the standard courses, day trips and live-aboards from its Beach Centre location in Kata. The PADI Open

Water course costs 11,900B. (📞095 441 665; www.rumblefishadventure.com; 98/79 Beach Centre, Th Kata, Hat Kata; 2/3 dives 2900/3700B; ⏱10am-7pm)

Aspasia SPA

13 ⊙ Map p58, C4

An excellent day spa is hidden in this Mexican-esque condo resort in the headland between Kata and Karon. The Zen interior is polished, with rice-paper doors. Try the fusion massage blending Eastern and Western techniques, the coffee blossom body scrub or an after-sun body wrap. The stellar sea views are worth the steep hike from the main Karon–Kata road. (📞076 333033; www.aspasiaphuket.com; 1/3 Th Laem Sai, Hat Kata; massage 1520-2570B; ⏱10am-8pm)

Dino Park GOLF

14 ⊙ Map p58, C4

Jurassic Park meets minigolf at this bizarre fun park on the southern edge of Hat Karon. It's a maze of caves, bars, waterfalls, lagoons, leafy gardens and dinosaur statues, all spread across 18 holes of putting greens. Kids will have a blast, but really it's for everyone. (📞076 330625; www.dinopark.com; Th Karon/Patak West, Hat Karon; adult/child 240/180B; ⏱10am-11pm)

Infinite Luxury Spa SPA

15 ⊙ Map p58, C6

Tucked into Kata's hottest new luxury resort is this uber-modern innovative

Top Tip

Beach Club Bookings

Catering to the fashionable and affluent, Phuket's contentiously popular beach clubs come under huge demand during peak season. If you fancy a day of luxury sandside lounging amid faux leather, ritzy cabanas and background bass, it's best to reserve a spot a week ahead. During low season, however, there are huge discounts, and you'll have plenty of space to yourself – probably without even booking.

spa that blends traditional therapies with bang-up-to-date technology that includes an anti-jetlag pod and a colour-changing 'chakra room'. Treatments range from the classic Thai massage to bioenergy mud-wraps, couples' oil massages and 'marine-flora' facials. It's pricey, no doubt about it, but perfect for a splurge. (📞076 370 777; www.katarocks.com; Kata Rocks, 186/22 Th Koktanod, Hat Kata; massage 4200B; ⏱10am-10pm)

Dive Asia DIVING

16 ⊙ Map p58, C4

Runs an extensive range of PADI certification courses (Open Water 11,600B to 16,020B) plus day-trip dives to Ko Phi-Phi and live-aboards to the Similan and Surin Islands (from 21,000B). (📞076 330 598; www.diveasia.com; 24 Th Karon, Hat Kata; 2/3 dives 3400/3900B; ⏱10am-9pm)

Eating

Boathouse Wine & Grill
INTERNATIONAL $$$

The perfect place to wow a special date (see 8 Map p58, D6), this is the pick of the bunch for many a local foodie. The atmosphere can feel a little old-school stuffy, but it's all very glam – plus the Thai and Mediterranean food (think: tiger prawn risotto and lobster soufflè) is fabulous, the wine list famously expansive and the sea views sublime. Special sharing platters are prepared at your table. (☏076 330015; www.boathousephuket.com; 182 Th Koktanod, Hat Kata; mains 470-1750B; tasting menu 1800-2200B; ⊙11am-10.30pm)

Pad Thai Shop
THAI $

17 ✘ Map p58, D4

This glorified roadside food shack does rich, savoury chicken stew and absurdly good *kôw pàt bóo* (crab fried rice), *pàt see·éw* (fried noodles) and noodle soup. It also serves up some of the best *pàt tai* we've ever tasted: spicy and sweet, packed with tofu, egg and peanuts, and plated with a side of spring onions, beansprouts and lime. Don't miss the house-made chilli sauces. (Th Patak East, Hat Karon; dishes 50B; ⊙9am-6pm)

Capannina
ITALIAN $$

18 ✘ Map p58, D6

Everything at this modern semi-open-air eatery – from pastas to sauces – is made fresh. Service can be inconsistent, but the four-cheese ravioli is memorable, the risotto comes highly recommended, and there are excellent pizzas, calzones and bruschettas, plus weekly specials on the board. It gets crowded during the high season, so you may want to book ahead. (☏076 284318; www.capannina-phuket.com; 30/9 Mu 2, Th Kata, Hat Kata; mains 160-800B; ⊙11am-11pm Nov-Apr, 5.30-11pm May-Oct)

Mom Tri's Kitchen
FUSION, MEDITERRANEAN $$$

A 'special occasion' or intimate lunch splash-out, Mom Tri's Kitchen offers fusion haute cuisine and fine wines. Diners pick from a hugely varied Mediterranean menu that loops local ingredients into its exquisite dishes, such as blue crab soufflé, lemongrass-infused sea bass and rock lobster ravioli in white wine, while overlooking beautiful Hat Kata Noi from a sensational cliff-side perch. (see 9 Map p58, C7; ☏076 333569; www.villaroyalephuket.com; 12 Th Kata Noi, Hat Kata Noi; mains 630-1660B; ⊙7am-11.30pm; P✏)

Kata Mama
THAI $

Our pick of several cheapie seafood huts hidden at the southern end of Hat Kata Yai (see 10 Map p58, C6), Kata Mama keeps busy thanks to its charming management, reliably tasty Thai standards and low-key beachside setting. (Hat Kata Yai; mains 50-400B; ⊙8am-9pm)

Mom Tri's Kitchen

Red Chopsticks
THAI $$

19 Map p58, C4

This fun contemporary-Thai eatery, just beyond south Hat Karon, is a welcome breath of sophistication. Dine in a smart, fashionable food lounge full of cosy striped chairs, thick wood pillars and dangling low-light lamps, where busy waiters deliver clay-pot seafood grills, light bubbling curries and herb-infused stir-fries from the open-plan kitchen. The cocktail list is suitably exhaustive. (076 330625; Th Karon, Hat Karon; mains 80-250B; noon-midnight;)

Mama Noi's
THAI, ITALIAN $

20 Map p58, C3

This simple cafe with faded Italy photos, a good local vibe and dangling pot plants has been feeding the expat masses for a generation. It does fantastic versions of all the Thai dishes plus a huge list of popular pastas – anyone for red-curry spaghetti? Cheap, tasty and friendly. (Karon Plaza, Hat Karon; mains 90-185B; 9am-10pm;)

Kampong Kata Hill
THAI $$

21 Map p58, C4

Spread across two peaceful, intimate pavilions, this excellent little eatery overflows with traditional teak wood, Thai antiques and softly tinkling music. Sure, it's a little catered towards tourists, but it's undeniably atmospheric, has on-the-ball staff, enjoys broad Kata views, and serves some fabulous local dishes and seafood, including lobster specials. Access is via a long, concrete stairway; there's no lift. (☑076 330103; 4 Th Karon/Patak West, Hat Kata; mains 230-500B; ☺6-10.30pm)

Kwong Shop Seafood
THAI, SEAFOOD **$$**

 22 Map p58, C4

Who doesn't love a time-worn fish shack? Using enticing displays of fresh seafood and snaps of blissed-out diners as bait, this cheap and cheerful old-school Thai joint has been reeling in hungry customers for over 25 years. (66 Th Thai Na, Hat Kata; mains 100-600B; ☺noon-10pm)

Karon Seafood
THAI **$$**

23 Map p58, C1

This seafood-dominated spot is definitely not off the beaten track, but sometimes that's OK. Hordes descend for delicacies such as curry-fried crab, lemon-steamed white snapper and prawns in yellow curry powder. It also does feast-style mixed-grilled seafood sharing platters (450B to 1150B). (514 Mu 1, Th Patak East, Hat Karon; mains 250-450B; ☺8am-midnight)

Bai Toey
THAI **$$**

 24 Map p58, C1

A charming Thai bistro with shaded outdoor patio and tasteful indoor seating. It has the traditional curry, stir-fry and noodle dishes, and excellent Thai-style grilled beef. (☑081 691 6202; www.baitoeyrestaurant.com; 192/36 Th Karon; mains 150-350B; ☺9am-11pm; 🛜)

Two Chefs
INTERNATIONAL **$**

25 Map p58, D6

Two Chefs continues to take over Kata, Karon and Kamala, but this original (just inland from the south end of Hat Kata Yai) remains the favourite. It's your classic bar and grill with plenty of live music, cheap booze and comfort food. Get stuck in with creamy mushroom pasta, pesto-filled bacon-wrapped chicken breast or a 200g Australian beef tenderloin burger. (☑076 333370; www.twochefs.com; 243 Th Koktanod/Patak West, Hat Kata ; mains 295-795B; ☺8am-11.30pm; 🛜)

Drinking

Ska Bar
BA

Tucked into rocks on the southernmost curl of Hat Kata Yai (see 10 Map p58; C6) and seemingly intertwined with the trunk of a grand old banyan tree, Ska is our choice for seaside sundowners. The Thai bartenders add to the laid-back Rasta vibe, and buoy paper lanterns and flags dangle from the canopy. Hang around if there's a

Understand
The Big Phuket Beach Clean-Up

As of Thailand's 2014 military takeover, the governing Thai junta has been tackling Phuket's notoriously widespread corruption. Most noticeably, this has involved a firm crackdown on illegal construction and consumer activity on the island's overcrowded beaches, and on its 'taxi mafia'(p30).

Initially, all rental sunbeds, deckchairs and umbrellas were banned, with thousands removed under the watch of armed soldiers. Vendors, masseuses and restaurants on the sand were ordered off the beach. Illegally encroaching buildings were bulldozed, including well-established beach clubs and restaurants, and others dramatically reduced in size.

How does all this affect travellers? At the time of writing, beach mats and umbrellas are still available to rent, in limited numbers and in '10%' allocated areas; sunbeds remain banned. Tourists may pitch their own umbrellas and chairs within the '10%' zone. Of course, people aren't necessarily following these new regulations. Jet skis, which were suspended to begin with, are still very much operating on Patong and Kamala. Some businesses have defied close-down orders and popped back up elsewhere.

For now, you'll be enjoying Phuket's beautiful beaches in refreshingly tidier, less-hassle versions, albeit with more limited amenities. This is a trial run that may be extended to other parts of the country and the situation is complex and open to change.

ire show. (www.skabar-phuket.com; 186/12 h Koktanod; ☼noon-late)

After Beach Bar   BAR

26   Map p58, D7

t's impossible to overstate how glorious the 180-degree views are from this stilted, thatched reggae bar clinging to a cliff above Kata: rippling sea, rocky peninsulas and palm-dappled hills. Now wack on the Bob Marley and you've got the perfect sunset-watching spot. When the fireball finally drops, ights from fishing boats blanket the horizon. It also does some flavour-

bursting pàt tai. (☎081 894 3750; Rte 4233; ☼9am-10.30pm)

Mr Pan's Art Space   BAR

27   Map p58, D5

Hands down the most fabulously quirky bar in Phuket, Mr Pan's is a trippy multi-use space bursting with colour and smothered in uniquely brushed canvases and sculptures celebrating, especially, the feminine form. It's the work of an eccentric creative and his tattoo-artist wife, who also whip up simple meals (160B to 400B). There's regular live music around 8pm. (Th Kade Kwan, Hat Kata; ⏰11am-11pm)

Italian Job   CAFE

28 🚇 Map p58, D6

A contemporary-style Italian coffee lounge with wi-fi, decent pastries, delicious espresso, *limoncello* (Italian lemon liqueur) and a loyal morning following. It overlooks a busy junction – perfect for people watching from air-conditioned comfort. (www.facebook.com/italianjobcoffeekata; 179/1 Th Koktanod, Hat Kata; ⏰8am-9.30pm; 🛜)

Angus O'Tool's   PUB

29 🚇 Map p58, C1

Tucked into a tatty soi at the north end of Karon, this dark, authentic

> #### Understand
> ### Rip Currents
>
> Rip currents (commonly known as 'rips') are the number one danger for tourists visiting Phuket's beaches. During the May to October monsoon, large waves and fierce undertows sometimes make it too dangerous to swim. Dozens of drownings occur every year on Phuket's beaches, especially throughout the rainy season and on Laem Singh, Hat Kamala, Hat Karon and Hat Patong. Red flags are posted to warn bathers of serious rips: don't swim in the red-flagged areas!

Irish pub beams all the big Premier League, Aussie Rules, rugby and cricket games, and has Guinness, Magners and Kilkenny on tap. It has classic pub fare of jacket potatoes, bangers and mash (mains 280B to 495B) and big greasy breakfasts. (📞093 696 1718; www.otools-phuket.com; 516/19 Th Patak East, Hat Karon; ⏰10am-1am; 🛜)

Palm Square   BA

30 🚇 Map p58, D5

Building local heritage into modernity, Palm Square is a fresh, glitzy entertainment complex inspired by Phuket's gorgeous Sino-Portuguese architecture. Inside you'll find a multilevel mishmash of Thai and international eateries, mod cafes, massage parlours, a yoga centre and, of course, a good sprinkling of bars with sports screens, open-air lounges and live music thrown into the mix. (www.palmsquarephuket.com; 88/29-30 Th Kata/Patak West, Hat Kata; ⏰8am-midnight)

Shopping

Baru   FASHIO

31 🔒 Map p58, C4

A stunning collection of exotic prints light fabrics, sparkly accessories, leather bags, elegant dresses and bold-coloured bikinis make Baru a hi with its fashion-conscious devotees. This is what Phuket's signature East-meets-West island style is all about. (📞076 333237; www.barufashion.com; Th Karon/Patak West, Hat Karon; ⏰9am-11pm)

Ska Bar (p66)

iam Handicraft · CLOTHING

2 🔒 Map p58, C4

his boho-chic store specialises in
andwoven linen dresses, shirts,
hawls, trousers and other men's
nd women's fashion, mostly locally
ade with hemp and organic cot-
n, and stocks a lovely collection
f silver and beaded jewellery. (www.
cebook.com/Siam-Handicraft-Phuket-Thai
nd-133750519986708; 12 Th Karon/Patak
est, Hat Karon; ⏰10am-10pm)

arin Waris · BEAUTY

elcome to an organic wonderland of
omemade tropical-fruit-based beauty,
ody and hair products. Concoct your
wn DIY spa session from the likes of
egg yolk and papaya shampoo, avocado scrub, mangosteen moisturiser and
coconut soaps on a rope to keep silky
soft and soothe sun-inflicted woes.
(see 32 🔒 Map p58, C4; www.facebook.
com/Parin-Waris-Thai-Organic-Phuket-Thai
land-154010827959836; 14 Th Karon/Patak
West, Hat Karon; ⏰10am-11pm)

La Banana · FASHION

Because one bikini is never enough.
Fall into this teensy boutique (see 32
🔒 Map p58, C4) to stock up on skimpy,
affordable two-pieces in a rainbow
of colours, styles and patterns, plus
floaty beachwear and cute dresses for
casually draping over the top. (Th Kata/
Patak West, Hat Karon; ⏰11am-10pm)

Explore

Rawai

Now this is a place to live. Phuket's rapidly developing south coast is teeming with retirees, artists, and Thai and expat entrepreneurs. The island's original tourist destination, Rawai doesn't obviously embody beach-bum bliss, but has hidden beauties. Visit for the laid-back vibe, seafood grills and lush coastal hills tumbling into the Andaman forming Laem Phromthep, Phuket's southernmost point.

The Region in a Day

Life is all about kicking back in Rawai, so start off late with pancakes or pastries at the **German Bakery** (p78). Devote an hour or two to soaking up the spiritual atmosphere at **Wat Chalong** (p77), then head straight to **Hat Ya Nui** (p75) or **Ao Sane** (p76) for a slice of pristine mountain-backed beach minus the crowds. For lunch, seek out spectacularly positioned **Sabai Corner** (p77).

Go for an action-packed afternoon kitesurfing off Hat Friendship with **Kite Zone** (p76) or horse riding through jungle with **Phuket Riding Club** (p76). Otherwise, take it slow checking out the vibrant art at **Phuket Art Village** (p76). For sensational sunset views, make your way to **Laem Phromthep** (p72), arguably the island's finest viewpoint.

Once the sun sinks, ease into Rawai's balmy laid-back evenings. Feast on seafood at one of the beachfront grills (p80), or get stuck into rich pasta and New Zealand lamb shanks at thatch-roofed **Rum Jungle** (p77). While away the night with cocktails on the rocky waterfront at **Nikita's** (p80), then party on at **Laguna Rawai** (p81).

Top Experiences
Laem Phromthep (p72)

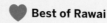 Best of Rawai

Dining
Da Vinci (p78)

Baan Rimlay (p79)

German Bakery (p78)

Drinking & Nightlife
Nikita's (p80)

Laguna Rawai (p81)

Getting There

Sŏrng·tăa·ou From 7am to 5.30pm, *sŏrng·tăa·ou* (passenger pick-up trucks) run from Phuket Town's Th Ranong to Rawai (40B). Some continue to Hat Nai Han (40B), but not all, so ask first.

Taxi Private taxis go from Rawai and Hat Nai Han to the airport (750B), Patong (700B) and Phuket Town (500B). Taxis from Rawai to Nai Han cost 200B.

Top Experiences
Laem Phromthep

This is it: Phuket's southernmost point. If you want to see the luscious Andaman Sea bend around the island and shimmer into the distance beyond, come to outrageously scenic Laem Phromthep. You won't be alone, but once you scan the 270 degrees of Andaman Sea, noticing how elegantly it arcs around the cape below, where local fishers cast into the whooshing waves from jutting rocks, that won't matter. You might even enjoy the catchy communal buzz.

Map p74, A4

Rte 4233

admission free

Lighthouse at Laem Phromthep

Don't Miss

The Views

There's a reason why busloads of tourists and packs of Phuketians descend on buzzy Laem Phromthep every afternoon. From the hilltop viewpoint, you'll enjoy panoramic vistas over the southern tip of Phuket, northwest to Hat Nai Han and across the tropical turquoise waters of the island-dotted Andaman. But the pink-tinged sunset is the real reason to visit. People sprawl on the grass or perch atop the palm-lined concrete wall to bask in the final moments of warmth, before the sun drops into the sea.

Elephant Shrine

On the central platform above the car park sits a small, evocative elephant shrine encircled by hundreds of wooden, ceramic and gold-painted elephant statues in all kinds of sizes and adorned with rich-coloured flowers. The elephants represent wisdom and strength in the Buddhist teaching, and local believers pray here.

Lighthouse

Topped by two golden elephants, Laem Phromthep's lighthouse was built in 1996 to commemorate the Golden Jubilee of King Bhumibol Adulyadej. From the very top, you'll gain an elevated view of the sunset and, usually, more exciting photo opportunities away from the crowds. Out the front of the lighthouse, there's a handy information board detailing the time of the sunrise and sunset for the day and the date.

☑ Top Tips

▶ At sunset, the photo-snapping hordes descend in luxury buses. If you crave privacy, take the faint, steep fishers' trail downhill to the rocky peninsula and watch the sun drop in a more peaceful environment.

▶ If you want to avoid the crowds completely, arrive around 4pm. You'll get to appreciate the views in more solitude, grab a drink and head back for sunset.

▶ Note that smoking and alcohol are not allowed on the viewpoint.

✖ Take a Break

With red-clad tables dotted across the hillside and its flower-filled gardens, chill music and beautiful sea panoramas, **Phromthep Cape Restaurant** (☏076 288656; 94/6 Th Viset, Mu 6, Laem Phromthep; mains 120-300B; ☺10am-10pm) is lovely for a bite. Dine on refined Italian fare at open-air **Da Vinci** (p78), 4km northeast.

For reviews see

◉ Top Experiences	p72
◉ Experiences	p75
✗ Eating	p77
◐ Drinking	p80

Experiences

Hat Nai Han BEACH

1 ◎ Map p74, B3

Ask a Phuket local or expat which their favourite beach is and they should say Hat Nai Han, though they'll probably send you off somewhere else and keep this one to themselves. One of Rawai's great swimming spots (be careful of rips in low season), this is a beautifully curved white crescent on the west side of the cape, with minimal development and backed by casuarinas and a seafront wát.

Hat Ya Nui BEACH

2 ◎ Map p74, B4

About 700m north of Laem Phromthep, tucked between the cape and Hat Nai Han where the road dips back down to the sea, is this gorgeous mellow cove with a healthy rocky snorkelling reef. Hat Ya Nui is the quintessential turquoise bay, with jungled mountains behind and an island dominating the horizon. It's a deservedly popular sunset-watching spot too. (Rte 4233)

Secret Viewpoint VIEWPOINT

3 ◎ Map p74, B3

For a sensational sunset view that doesn't involve jostling through the crowds at Laem Phromthep, seek out this more secluded spot 1.5km north of the cape on Rte 4233. At the top of the hill there is a turn-off to a small gazebo, where you can sit on the sloping grass while the sun sinks. There'll be a few tourists and locals around, and you'll have an outrageous north- and west-facing panorama sans tour buses. (Rte 4233)

Rawai Supa Muay Thai THAI BOXING

4 ◎ Map p74, D2

Strap up those wrists and get fired up at this Thai boxing gym opened by a former *moo·ay tai* champion (he doesn't teach here). People come from around the world to learn how to fight alongside seasoned Thai professionals. It's a mix of Thais and foreigners who live in on-site dorms, but tourists can join drop-in classes and yoga (400B). (☑076 226495; www.supamuaythaiphuket. com; 43/42 Mu 7, Th Viset; per session/week 300/3000B; ☺7am-7pm Mon-Sat, 9am-6pm Sun)

Karon Viewpoint VIEWPOINT

5 ◎ Map p74, B1

From this majestic clifftop lookout, views sprawl across Kata to the northern reaches of Karon and, to the south, wrap around the coast to Laem Phromthep. Come for sunset, though it's a beautiful spot at any time. Don't linger late at night; there have been reports of attacks and robberies in the wee hours. To get here from central Rawai, head 3.5km northwest on Rte 4233. (Hwy 4233, 2.5km south of Kata)

Hat Rawai

BEACH

6 Map p74, D3

Not really good for lounging, Hat Rawai is a rocky long-tail and speed-boat harbour with a string of seafood grills on the east side of the cape. This is where most of the luxury condo development seems to be proliferating.

Kite Zone

KITESURFING

7 Map p74, E1

Rawai is a fine place to tackle kitesurfing and this cool young school has a tremendous perch on Hat Friendship. Courses range from one-hour tasters to three-day, 10-hour courses. From April to October, classes happen at Hat Nai Yang (p109) on the north-west side of the island. Also rents kit (per hour/day 1200/3500B) and runs stand-up paddle trips (from 700B). (083 395 2005; www.kitesurfthailand.com; Hat Friendship; 1hr lesson 1100B, 3-day course 10,000-15,000B)

Ao Sane

BEACH

8 Map p74, B3

Just northwest from Hat Nai Han, on Rawai's west coast, you might well think the road dead-ends. Not true. Power on, passing Pier 93 Yacht Club and you'll wind 500m along the dramatic coast to the small but beautiful, boulder-strewn white-sand beach of Ao Sane. It's rugged and laid-back, enticing regular return visitors.

Phuket Art Village

ARTS CENTRE

9 Map p74, C2

A group of talented Thai artists clubbed together to set up this bohemian, banyan-shaded arts community, just off Rawai's main strip. Feel free to wander the wonderfully creative home-studio-galleries packed with (mostly) boldly contemporary original artwork in vibrant colours and, if you're lucky, meet resident artists. **Red Gallery**, with its dreamlike animal canvases, and **Love Art Studio**, crafted entirely from colour-washed reclaimed wood, are standouts. (095 026 6100, 089 471 5653; www.facebook.com/pages/Phuket-Art-Village/320158668080202; 28/68 Soi Naya 2, Th Viset; admission free; 10am-10pm, hours vary)

Phuket Riding Club

HORSE RIDING

10 Map p74, E1

The perfect opportunity to live out that horse-riding through the tropics dream. Phuket Riding Club offers fun one- and two-hour rides in the jungle around Rawai. Book a day ahead. (076 288213; www.phuketridingclub.com; 95 Th Viset; 1/2hr 1000B/2000B; 7.30am-6.30pm)

Sinbi Muay Thai

THAI BOXING

11 Map p74, C1

A well-respected boxing training camp for both men and women. (083 391 5535; www.sinbi-muaythai.com; 100/15 Mu 7, Th Sai Yuan; per session/week 400/4800B; 7.30am-7pm Mon-Sat)

Atsumi

SPA

12 Map p74, D1

Phuket isn't all about boozing and gorging on cream-loaded curries. In fact, there's a flourishing wellness scene. At this earthy fasting-detox retreat, guests check in for days-long water, juice and/or herb fasts with massages. The regularly eating public is welcome for spa sessions, taking in traditional Thai, oil and deep-tissue treatments, plus signature Thaiatsu massages (Thai meets shiatsu) and yoga (300B). (☑081 272 0571; www. atsumihealing.com; 34/18 Soi Pattana, Th Sai Yuan; massage 600-1000B, treatment 1200-1600B; ☺9am-5pm)

Phuket Shooting Range Complex

ADVENTURE SPORTS

13 Map p74, E1

Swing by this action-packed 'playground' for adults for an astounding array of active entertainment that includes archery, a shooting gallery, go-karting, ATV adventures and paintball spread out across the complex. (☑076 381667; 82/2 Th Patak East, Rte 4028; go-karting per 10min from 890B, shooting gallery 10 shots from 1180B; ☺9am-6pm)

Eating

Rum Jungle

INTERNATIONAL $$$

14 Map p74, C1

One of Rawai's finest, this semi-open thatched-roof restaurant with an

 Local Life

Wat Chalong

Catch a glimpse of local life at **Wat Chalong** (วัดฉลอง; www.wat-chalong-phuket.com; Rte 4021; admission by donation; ☺7am-5pm; **P**), 3km north of Chalong circle. This three-tiered salmon-pink temple has 36 golden Buddhas seated, reclining and meditating around its elaborate exterior. Green-and-gold *naga* line its banisters and the lotus ponds behind. Though not an antique, it definitely possesses a spiritual vibration, especially when worshippers pay their respects. Busloads of visitors pour in, so swing by in the early morning for a chance of tranquility. Please dress respectfully.

exceptional world-beat soundtrack is family run and spearheaded by a terrific Aussie chef. The New Zealand lamb shank is divine, as are the steamed clams, and the pasta sauces are all made from scratch. Tempting veggie choices include aubergine parmigiana and pasta Gorgonzola. (☑076 388153; www.facebook.com/Rum-Jungle-Cafe-Rawai-Phuket-173738946050909; 69/8 Mu 1, Th Sai Yuan; mains 240-620B; ☺11.30am-2pm & 6-10.30pm; ☑)

Sabai Corner

INTERNATIONAL, THAI $$

15 Map p74, A1

There's no better Phuket view than the one from this wide deck: all the way to Karon in one direction and an endless horizon of blue ocean in the other. This popular Swiss-American-Thai-owned indoor-outdoor eatery is a stellar nature-fringed find frequented by local expats. From central Rawai, head 3.5km northwest towards Kata on Rte 4233, turn downhill immediately before Karon Viewpoint and drive 1.5km. (089 875 5525; www.facebook.com/Sabai-Corner-150517525037992; off Rte 4233; mains 100-400B; 10am-10pm;)

Da Vinci
ITALIAN $$$

16 Map p74, C2

Alfresco wining and dining on crisp white-linen tables at this modern, authentic Italian kitchen is perfect on a balmy night. Staff are lovely and warm, the pizza is wood-fired, breads are fresh and pastas arrive full of flavour. The world-roaming wine list is excellent and there's complimentary after-dinner limoncello (lemon liqueur) up for grabs. Popular with families for the kids' play area. (076 289574; www.davinciphuket.com; 28/46 Mu 1, Th Viset; mains 320-900B; 5.30-10.30pm)

Top Tip

Boat Charters

Hat Rawai (Map p74, D3) is an excellent place to arrange boat charters to neighbouring islands. Destinations include nearby Ko Bon (long-tail/speedboat 1200/2400B) and Coral Island (1800/3500B) for quiet snorkelling; maximum eight passengers.

Som Tum Lanna
THAI $

17 Map p74, D1

When it comes to *sôm·dam* (spicy green papaya salad), order it mild – it'll still bring some serious heat. And while the fish at this Isan soul food shack is good, its equal exists elsewhere. The chicken on the other hand is outstanding. (081 597 0569; 3/7 Th Sai Yuan, Hat Rawai; mains 80-150B; 9am-5pm Tue-Sun)

German Bakery
EUROPEAN $

18 Map p74, C2

This fun, friendly restaurant run by a German-Thai couple does the best pastries in the area. It makes fine brown bread, serves excellent breakfasts (try the pineapple pancakes), and has amazing bratwurst and sauerkraut. Surfers come here to fuel up before an early session. (Th Viset; mains 80-140B; 7.30am-4.30pm)

A Spoonful of Sugar
CAFE $

19 Map p74, C2

Practically everything at this sweet, whitewashed cafe coated in flowery prints is wholesome and tasty. Wholemeal pancakes are topped with mango or kiwi and yoghurt, and there's a long list of coffees, smoothies, juices and even protein shakes. Laze in the air-con lounge or on the wraparound veranda. (076 388432; www.facebook.com/spoonfulofsugar; 30/10 Mu 1, Th Viset; dishes 50-150B; 8am-7pm Tue-Sun)

Seafood stalls on the beach, Rawai

Banana Corner

THAI $

20 ✕ Map p74, D1

A laid-back little tucked-away spot, Banana Corner dishes up delicious, affordable Thai fare in a lush, twinkling, tropical garden hidden behind a low-key bar. Nothing fancy, but its rich *pá·naang* curry and fluffy *kôw pàt pak* (veg fried rice) are both excellent. (www.facebook.com/pages/Banana-Corner-Rawai-Phuket/1039879679362901; 43/47 Th Sai Yuan; mains 90-300B; ☺12.30-11pm; P)

Baan Rimlay

THAI $$

21 ✕ Map p74, D3

This shady Thai seafood house immediately southwest of Rawai's pier steams clams, mussels and fish, and grills squid, prawns and lobster to perfection. For something light, try the terrific seafood salads. The seafood is a tad pricier here than at humbler seafood eateries nearby, but the seaside location and views are exceptional. It *can* get busy with loud tour groups. (Th Viset, Hat Rawai; mains 120-400B; ☺10am-10pm; P)

Crepes Village

FRENCH $$

22 ✕ Map p74, C2

A fairy-lit pebbled garden with wooden gazebos, this family-friendly French-owned eatery does tasty French-Thai fusion crepes in sweet and savoury styles. You'll find classics such as egg, ham and cheese, and

Suzette, but brave a local twist with red-chicken-curry or *pá·naang goong* (*pá·naang* curry prawns with coconut milk and basil) crepes. Keep things fruity and tropical with choices filled with pineapple, coconut or mango. (📞085 655 7329; 28/31 Mu 1, Th Viset; mains 160-220B; ⏲10am-10pm; 👶)

Natural Efe Macrobiotic World
VEGETARIAN, VEGAN $$

23 ✖ Map p74, C2

This chilled-out health-food kitchen plates up such organic, sugar-free vegetarian and vegan delights as tofu sandwiches, dried-fruits-and-quinoa salad and lentil soup, at wooden tables set around a pool in its cute back courtyard. Also on offer is a wide selection of freshly squeezed 'super-juices', health drinks (hemp milk?) and teas. (📞089 785 4801; 14/93-94 Mu 1, Th Viset; mains 100-250B; ⏲9am-7pm; 🖊)

Local Life
Rawai's Seafood Grills

Hat Rawai is lined with over a dozen locally owned, wonderfully priced **seafood grills** (mains 90B to 300B; ⏲10am to 10pm), sizzling with fresh catch along the roadside promenade, with seating on plastic chairs or blankets on the floor. It doesn't really matter which one you choose. All the fish is fresh, as are the crab, clams, mussels, squid, lobster and tiger prawns. Make sure you try the spicy sauce, not that sweet and sour syrup.

Oyjoi Number 1 Thai Food
THAI $

24 ✖ Map p74, C3

Don't let humble roots fool you. This delightful garden cafe run out of the chef's front yard serves some delicious Thai food: searing *pá·naang* curry (clotted with coconut cream), sticky tamarind prawns and spicy fish soup. (📞081 884 4033; 83/40 Mu 2, Th Viset; mains 90-180B; ⏲noon-9.30pm)

Drinking

Nikita's
BAR

This beautifully chilled-out open-air hang-out gazes over the sea just west of Rawai's pier (see 21 ✖ Map p74, D3), with coffee, green tea and a good selection of shakes and cocktails. A mango margarita, perhaps? If you're hungry, it also does decent watering-hole food such as omelettes, pastas, burgers and wood-fired pizzas. (📞076 288703; www.nikitas-phuket.com; Hat Rawai; mains 150-350B; ⏲10am-midnight; 📶)

Pier 93 Yacht Club
BAR

25 🍷 Map p74, B3

Sailing flags flap in the ocean breeze, waves pound the rock below and there's nothing in sight but turquoise sea and island views from this elegant yacht-club patio bar. It's a location that demands a beverage. And another one after that. From November to May, a floating jetty host hundreds of boats. (📞098 374 9205; 11/11 Hat Nai Han; ⏲4pm-midnight)

Reggae Bar BAR

26 🚆 Map p74, C2

Spilling out from an old wooden shed is this creatively cluttered, laid-back lounge bobbing to classic roots tunes. A leathersmiths by day, it hosts impromptu jams and erratic concerts, barbecues and parties, featuring local reggae bands and, occasionally, some of Thailand's most legendary Rastas. Leather belts dangle, art is plastered across walls, and blacklight graffiti covers every inch of space. (Th Viset; 🕙noon-late, hours vary)

Lavinier Coffee CAFE

27 🚆 Map p74, C2

Logo look familiar? This local incarnation of Starbucks is a good spot to kick back for a while over a good coffee made from ground Arabica beans sourced from Chiang Mai. Thai-Croatian-run, it also serves traditional homemade breads, European pastry favourites and egg breakfasts featuring vegetable or ham frittata. (www. laviniercoffee.com; 15/39 Mu 1, Th Viset; 🕙8am-7pm; 🛜)

Laguna Rawai CLUB

28 🚆 Map p74, D3

One of few late-night spots in mellow Rawai, Laguna sprawls across a club and a bunch of bars opposite each other off southern Th Viset (on east-coast Rawai). Things get busy on weekend nights, attracting a mixed crowd of Thais, foreigners and bar girls after knock off. Bars go from 9pm to 2am, then everyone falls into the club. Sip cocktails and showcase your pool-playing talent. (www. lagunarawai.com; Th Viset; admission free; 🕙9pm-5am; 🛜)

Understand
Road Safety

There have been late-night motor-bike & muggings and stabbings on the road leading from Patong to Karon and from Kata to the Rawai–Hat Nai Han area, especially between Karon Viewpoint and Hat Nai Han. Most recent attacks have involved solo motorbike riders being pushed off their bikes and then robbed, and happened after midnight, so avoid driving in the wee hours.

Flip Side BEER GARDEN

29 🚆 Map p74, D3

Fresh-on-the-scene Flip Side is Rawai's craft-beer go-to spot. This smartly modern indoor-outdoor bar stocks an impressive line-up of over 40 Thai and international craft beers, with particular emphasis on Belgian and US labels. Gourmet beef burgers arrive on wooden platters. Nachos, sandwiches and other bites are available too (dishes 150B to 390B). (www.facebook. com/flipsidethailand; 469/4 Th Viset, Hat Rawai; 🕙11.30am-10.30pm Wed-Mon)

Explore

Hat Kamala & Hat Surin

Providing the perfect antidote to Patong's madness, the beautiful, creamy-blonde neighbouring beaches of Kamala and Surin are blessed with exquisite pale turquoise waters and gentle shore breakers. Chilled-out Kamala attracts lower-key visitors, while Surin revels in a glitzy party vibe. Despite luxury development, these sands suit friends, families and young couples, and remain grounded by rustic beachfront seafood shacks.

The Region in a Day

☀ Enjoy an Italian-infused breakfast at **Bocconcino** (p88), before claiming your white-sand turf on **Hat Kamala** (p85) or **Hat Surin** (p85), or splashing out on the full beach pampering experience at super-chic **Catch Beach Club** (p85). For those in Kamala, stroll past the beautiful, serene **Tsunami Memorial** (p85).

☀ Take a break from the scorching midday sun to lunch on Thai-Mediterranean fusion fare at **Taste** (p87) or with the sea breeze at simple Thai **Meena Restaurant** (p87). Then pop over to tucked-away **Laem Singh** (p85) for a late-afternoon dip or escape the heat with a pampering session at **Sun Spa** (p86). Activity lovers can hire a surfboard or take a surfing class.

☾ Top up your beachy island wardrobe at swish Surin boutiques such as **Chandra** (p90) and **Island Bliss** (p90), glam up for a delicious international dinner at **Catch** (p87), and finish off with wine, beer and cocktails next door at **Bimi Beach Club** (p89). If you're in Kamala, head to **Vanilla Sky** (p89) for cocktails high above the bay.

 Best of Hat Kamala & Hat Surin

Dining
Catch (p87)

Taste (p87)

Meena Restaurant (p87)

Shopping
Chandra (p90)

Lemongrass House (p90)

Getting There

🚗 **Taxi** Private taxis from the airport to Hat Surin or Hat Kamala cost 700B.

Sŏrng·tăa·ou From 7am to 5pm, *sŏrng·tăa·ou* (passenger pick-up trucks) run from Phuket Town's Th Ranong to Surin/Kamala (30/35B). They also go between Kamala and Surin (20B).

Túk-túk From Phuket Town to Hat Surin or Hat Kamala costs 500B. Surin to Kamala is about 200B.

A   B   C   D

Zazada
Beach
Club
8

Sun Spa
6

Catch
Beach
Club
2

7   Th Srisoonthorn

18   16

4025

Hat Surin
Hat Surin   Mandarin
Massage
20   19

3   **10**

12

Laem
Singh
Laem
Singh   **1**

4025

1

ANDAMAN
SEA

11

For reviews see

◉ Experiences	p85
✕ Eating	p87
◖ Drinking	p87
⌂ Shopping	p90

17

Hat
Kamala   **15**
4

Hat
Kamala

0   500 m
0   0.25 miles

Tsunami **5**
Memorial   **9**

Sŏrng·tǎa·ou
to Hat Surin &
Phuket Town

4233

Th Hat Kamala

Oasis
Spa   **13**

Soi 8

Th Nakalay

14

xperiences

em Singh
BEACH

⊙ Map p84, B2

cal beach addicts will tell you that
ff-framed Laem Singh, 1km north of
mala, conceals one of the island's
st beautiful beaches. Park on the
adland and clamber down a steep
ngle-frilled path, or you could
arter a long-tail (1000B) from Hat
mala. It gets crowded.

tch Beach Club
BEACH CLUB

⊙ Map p84, B1

ere's a day at the beach, and then
ere's a day at Catch – *the* place to
seen (preferably with a suntan)
Surin. Slip into your swankiest
achwear for plush, party-vibe lazing
Surin's white sands overlooking
rfect blue waters. Day passes bag
u a mat, towel and pillow, plus food
d drink (up to 2000B). Excellent
ue outside high season. (☎076
567; www.catchbeachclub.com; Hat Surin;
 pass low/high season 1000/2000B;
9am-2am)

at Surin
BEACH

⊙ Map p84, B1

ssy and stylish, Surin is the beach
ere resort-goers come to play.
uket's beach clean-up operation
s hit Surin particularly hard and, at
search time, all establishments on
 sand had been cleared away (leav-
; behind a slightly scruffy mess).

Despite this, Surin remains unpretentious, welcoming and beautiful, with
a village vibe, and makes a great spot
for a day frolicking on the sand. (👕)

Hat Kamala
BEACH

4 ⊙ Map p84, C4

Quiet and laid-back by Phuket standards, Hat Kamala is a well-enclosed
sugar-white strand with a rustic feel,
framed between green-clad headlands
and a spectacular turquoise bay. During the May-to-October monsoon, hire
surfboards (per hour 300B) and take
surfing classes (1500B) at its southern
end.

Tsunami Memorial
MEMORIAL

5 ⊙ Map p84, B5

Kamala was one of Phuket's worst
hit areas during the 2004 Boxing Day

Local Life

Masjid Mukaram Bang Thao

While not a must-see sight, this
busy **mosque** (Rte 4025; admission
free; ☉dawn-dusk) provides a good
insight into Phuket village life and
makes an interesting change of
scene from the beach. The bright-
white facade and sea-green mosaic
domes loom strikingly against
the blue sky and jungled hills, and
it's home to a friendly Muslim
population who set up tasty halal
street-food carts outside. Visitors
welcome.

Top Tip

Phuket Fantasea

It's impossible to ignore the brochures, billboards and touts flogging Phuket Fantasea, the US$60 million 'cultural theme park' just east of Hat Kamala, powerfully promoted as one of the island's top 'family-friendly' attractions. We recommend reading up on the numerous animal welfare issues associated with this Vegas-style spectacle, at which animals are forced to 'perform' daily, before choosing to support it. Consider treating kids to a more ecologically focused experience, such as the Phuket Gibbon Rehabilitation Project (p103), instead.

tsunami. The Heart of the Universe Memorial pays tribute to lost loved ones with a moving, wave-inspired metallic oval created by prominent Thai artist Udon Jiraksa. (Hat Kamala)

Sun Spa SPA

 6 Map p84, B1

Pamper yourself with a toning 'Qi Gong' facial, a tamarind body polish, a coconut milk bath and/or a candle-and-oils massage at this luxurious spa just back from the beach. It also has a full range of beauty services. The deluxe manicure comes highly recommended. (076 316500; www.twinpalms-phuket.com; Twin Palms, 106/46 Mu 3, Hat Surin; treatment 1500-2400B; ⏰11am-9pm)

Mandarin Massage SPA

7 Map p84, B1

A friendly, inexpensive massage parlour in clean, air-conditioned surrounds, with a short but sweet menu offering classic Thai massages and aloe vera massages for those who've roasted themselves under the sun. (081 614 1204; 106/38 Mu 3, Th Hat Surin, Hat Surin; massage 500B; ⏰9.30am-midnight)

Zazada Beach Club BEACH CLUB

8 Map p84, B1

On north Hat Surin you'll find one of the area's newest beach clubs. Not quite as glitzy as its neighbours, Zazada notches up points for its strikingly contemporary chilli-red pool and crimson-coated decor. Admission sees you kicking back on smart sunbeds (off the sand), and includes towels, pillows and water. Otherwise, drop in for mango mojitos and tasty (if pricey) Thai/international bites (340B to 640B). (076 386644; www.zazadabeachclub.com; Hat Surin; admission 300B; ⏰9am-midnight)

Oasis Spa SPA

9 Map p84, C5

Dainty water features and a classic Thai setting welcome you at this excellent upper-midrange day spa, with branches across Phuket. Tempting soothing treatments include signature hot-oil massages, Ayurvedic head massages, herbal clay wraps, and

hai coffee, honey and yoghurt body
crubs. Go for a package (from 3160B)
o pick and choose. (📞076 337777; www.
asisspa.net; 128 Mu 3, Hat Kamala; massage
400-3000B; ⏱10am-10pm)

Eating & Drinking

Catch
INTERNATIONAL $$$

Throw on your breeziest island-chic
outfit to dine overlooking the sea at
Surin's glitziest beach club (see 2
Map p84, B1). It's classy at every turn,
from ambience to cocktails and inter-
national cuisine (pastas, salads, burg-
ers, pizzas). Club admission (low/high
season 1000/2000B) buys you a beach
mat and pillow for the day, and goes
towards food and drinks. Or just grab
a table and order off the menu. (📞076
16567; www.catchbeachclub.com; Hat Surin;
mains 400-600B; ⏱noon-2am; 📶)

Taste
FUSION $$

Minimalist modern lines, top-notch
service, a sophisticated but chilled-out
vibe and delicious Thai-Mediterranean
fusion food make this urban-meets-
surf eatery an outstanding choice.
Dine indoors or alfresco on meal-sized
salads (try the goats' cheese with
smoked almonds), weekly specials
or a variety of creative starters and
mains. Ceramic fish swim above the
bathroom door. (📞076 270090; www.
tastesurinbeach.com; Hat Surin; dishes 200-
420B; ⏱noon-11pm Tue-Sun; 📶)

Meena Restaurant
THAI $

11 🍴 Map p84, C3

This family-run beachside shack
with rainbow-striped and leopard-
print sarongs for tablecloths is a real
find. The owners couldn't be more
welcoming. The tasty authentic Thai
food is exceptional and so are the
fresh fruit shakes. The rustic setting
is exactly what you (most likely) came
to Kamala for. It's at the north end of
the beach. (Hat Kamala; mains 80-150B;
⏱9am-5pm)

Twin Brothers
THAI $$

12 🍴 Map p84, B2

By day, one brother mans the wok,
stirring up decent seafood-focused
Thai food at (almost) local prices.
At night, the other fires up a fresh
seafood grill. It's more down to earth
than Surin's other options. (Hat Surin;
mains 120-350B; ⏱11am-10pm)

Top Tip

Surin Beach Cheap Eats

For cheap seafood in upmarket
Hat Surin, head to the numerous
delicious seafront dining rooms.
The most affordable eats are found
at the **food stalls** dotted around
the beachside parking lot and at
the couple of **roadside shacks**
heading inland on Rte 4025 (Th
Srisoonthorn).

Sugo
ITALIAN $$

A Sicilian chef leads this popular new 'rustic Italian' spot, 700m east of Hat Surin on Rte 4025 (see 20 🔒 Map p84, C1). It's smart and full of style, with specials chalked up on the walls. Slip into a bright-red booth or sneak into the back courtyard to feast on carefully crafted wood-fired pizza, pasta, bruschetta, meaty mains or antipasti platters. (📞076 386599; www.sugo-phuket. com; 117 Mu 3, Th Srisoonthorn, Hat Surin; mains 250-570B; ⏱5-10.30pm Tue-Sun)

Mam's Restaurant
THAI, INTERNATIONAL $$

13 Map p84, C5

There's no beach view, but local expats swear by this quiet, simple place with just a handful of tables sprinkled across the patio of a family home. Mam's plates up all the usual Thai suspects in meat, shrimp or veggie versions packed full of flavour, along with burgers, pastas, kebabs, sandwiches and, yes, even fish 'n' chips. It's about 400m east (inland) from the main highway. (📞089 032 2009; 32/32 Soi 8, Kamala; mains 90-280B; ⏱noon-10pm)

Plum
INTERNATIONAL $$$

14 ✕ Map p84, A5

Polished Mediterranean-Thai cuisine at this elegant hillside resort restaurant means light crispy salads, creamy risotto, seafood pasta, white-wine grilled salmon and Italian cheese platters, all generously served with beautiful beach and bay panoramas from up high. Book ahead to dine at an in-pool cabana table. (📞076 337300; Cape Sienna, 18/40 Mu 6, Th Nakalay, Hat Kamala; mains 400-1000B; ⏱6-11pm, close Mon May-Oct; ✒)

Deng's
INTERNATIONAL, THAI $

15 ✕ Map p84, C4

This welcoming semi-open eatery across the promenade from the sand serves some of the best food along central Hat Kamala. You'll find pasta, burgers and chicken breasts here, but you'd be better off savouring the local seafood. In high season, swing by from 7pm for the Wednesday barbecue buffet. (📞081 893 4094; www.dengs kamalabeachresort.com; Soi Police Station, Hat Kamala; mains 120-390B; ⏱8am-10pm)

Bocconcino
DELI, ITALIAN $$

16 ✕ Map p84, C1

An Italian deli may not be what you came to Phuket for, but Bocconcino's homemade gelato is classic Surin: refined and refreshing. This elegant, expat-frequented eatery houses an Italophile's dream of wines, coffee, cakes, cheeses, cured meats, homemade pastas, pizzas and changing specials. For something lighter, try traditional salads such as tomato and mozzarella. It's 600m east of Hat Surin. (📞076 386531; www.bocconcino phuket.com; 8/71 Mu 3, Th Srisoonthorn; mains 250-350B; ⏱9am-10pm; 📶)

Masjid Mukaram Bang Thao (p85)

Nanork Seafood THAI $$

  Map p84, C4

A charming stone and timber seafood restaurant with a daily mixed-grill selection and all your Thai classics served up at flowery-clothed tables tucked into a corner over the pavement from central Hat Kamala. Also rents surfboards (per hour 200B) and teaches surfing (per class 1500B). (☏081 978 6294; 94/19 Mu 3, Hat Kamala; mains 100-380B; ☺10am-10pm)

Bimi Beach Club BEACH CLUB

Brimming with fun vibes, Bimi (short for 'Bikinis & Martinis') has smashed-mosaic floors and a cascading indoor waterfall. Grab a Thai-jito full of Phuketian Chalong Bay Rum and sink into white-leather booths as the sun sets over the aqua Andaman (see 2 ◉ Map p84, B1). Good pastas, pizzas, salads and seafood plates too (mains 290B to 1500B). Daytime lounging passes cost 500/1000B in low/high season. (☏076 316580; www.bimibeachclub.com; Hat Surin; ☺10am-11pm; 🛜)

Vanilla Sky COCKTAIL BAR

Rustle up a colourful cocktail and watch the sun sink over the sea in style from what has to be Kamala's breeziest rooftop lounge (see 14 🍴 Map p84, A5; Cape Sienna, 18/40 Mu 6, Th Nakalay, Hat Kamala; ☺5pm-midnight)

Shopping

Chandra
FASHION

18 🔒 Map p84, C1

Fashionistas will adore this sparkly, sophisticated boutique that captures all that's young and glam about Phuket. Flick through rails of gorgeous, original beach-club-chic dresses, light kaftans, silk kimonos and bejewelled bikinis, designed in-house or sourced across Southeast Asia. Boys, it has linen shirts, silk-blend waistcoats and cotton tie-trousers. (📞082 274 8289; www.chandra-exotic.com; 8/44 Mu 3, Th Srisoonthorn, Hat Surin; ⏱10am-8pm)

Lemongrass House
BEAUTY

Phuket's top homegrown all-natural health and beauty producer, Lemongrass has shelves stacked high with moisturisers, creams, body scrubs, essential oils, chunky soaps, tropical shampoos, lip balms and body washes – all infused with delicious exotic ingredients from jasmine, green tea and papaya to its namesake lemongrass. Oh, and that nontoxic lavender and citronella mosquito repellent really does the job (see 7 ◉ Map p84, B1); 📞076 271233; www.lemongrasshouse.com; Th Hat Surin, Hat Surin; ⏱9.30am-8pm)

Island Bliss
FASHION

19 🔒 Map p84, C1

A classy high-end women's boutique specialising in bold, elegant beachwear style: flowing cotton maxi dresses in tasteful prints, colourful jewellery and tribal-print clutch bags. All are the creations of an Australian designer whose inspiration spans the world from Rajasthan to Ubud to Byron Bay. (📞076 621553; www.islandbliss phuket.com; 116 Mu 3, Th Srisoothorn, Hat Surin; ⏱10am-7pm)

Oriental Fine Art
ANTIQUES, ARTS

One of the best collections of traditional Southeast Asian art in Thailand, this museum-quality showroom displays a 3m Buddha encrusted with precious stones, an ancient teak shrine, terracotta sculptures, wooden Chinese furniture and other antique surprises. Absolutely everything is for sale. Swing by for a browse even if you aren't in the market. (see 7 ◉ Map p84, B1; 106/19-20 Th Hat Surin, Hat Surin; ⏱10am-7pm)

Soul of Asia
ARTS

20 🔒 Map p84, C1

A beautiful gallery filled with fine Southeast Asian modern and traditional art, mixed with a few antiques and original prints and lithographs from art masters such as Dalí and Miró. (📞076 270055; www.soulofasia.com; 5/50 Surin Plaza, Mu 3, Th Srisoonthorn, Hat Surin; ⏱10am-7pm)

Understand

The Plight of Phuket's Elephants

Although you don't have to travel far to meet Phuket's majestic elephants, the encounters on offer (rides and circus-like 'performances') are associated with complex animal welfare issues.

Illegal capture and trade to fuel the tourism industry are major threats to Thailand's dwindling wild elephant population: fewer than 2000 are thought to remain in the wild; an additional 3000 are 'domesticated'.

Many captured and captive-born elephants undergo a brutal process of being 'crushed' into submission via repetitive abuse, at great risk to the welfare of these gentle creatures.

Although trekking isn't inherently harmful to elephants, overloading their spines (which are weaker than commonly thought) is. Experts indicate adult elephants can comfortably carry up to 150kg at a time, for up to four hours a day; limits often exceeded at high-demand trekking camps. Elephant rides are incessantly flogged on Phuket. The island is home to 216 officially registered 'working' elephants, most of which live in camps, of varying quality, of up to 10 pachyderms. Hotels advertise elephant 'services' ranging from photo shoots to carting partygoers around.

Fortunately, Phuket is slowly experiencing a rise in demand for more responsible elephant interactions. In 2015 Phuket's now-closed Nikki Beach Club was internationally criticised for allowing drunk revellers to ride a baby elephant, and young Choojai was withdrawn from work at Marina Phuket following a high-profile online petition.

While boycotting elephant rides might seem like the obvious solution, the situation is complicated. Without tourist demand, and with Thailand's few sanctuaries currently unable to take in all of Thailand's mahouts and their charges, mahouts claim they (and their elephants) will have no source of income and sustenance.

While nothing beats observing an elephant in the wild (such as in Khao Sok National Park) conscientious travellers considering riding elephants should consider supporting more responsible outfits that provide safer working conditions for elephants. Indications that elephants are well cared for include bareback rides or custom-made wooden seats (instead of metal), a balanced diet, plenty of water, regular vet visits, non-excessive working hours, absence of wounds and a shady, social rest area.

Top Experiences
Big Buddha

Getting There

Big Buddha is an 11km drive east of Kata or Karon.

🚗 From Kata/Karon taxis cost 500B.

🚗 Drivers: it's 6km west off Rte 4021, 1km north of Chalong circle.

High atop the Nakkerd Hills, northwest of Chalong circle, and visible from almost half of the island, the 45m-high Big Buddha sits grandly on Phuket's finest viewpoint. It *can* feel more tourist-trap than spiritual haven, but the Buddha's sheer size and beauty, the awe-inspiring surrounds and the hilltop serenity are reason enough to linger a while. Pay your respects at the tin-roofed golden shrine, then climb the stairs to the Big Buddha itself.

Don't Miss

The Buddha

Construction began on Big Buddha in 2007. He's dressed in Burmese alabaster, which isn't cheap. All in all, the price tag is around 100 million baht (not that anybody minds). Phuketians refer to the Big Buddha as Phuket's most important project in the last 100 years, which means a lot considering that construction on Phuket hasn't stopped for the last 20 years.

The Views

From the Buddha's glorious plateau, peer into Kata's perfect turquoise bay, glimpse the shimmering Karon strand and, to the southeast, survey the pebble-sized channel islands of Chalong Bay. The serenity amid tinkling bells and yellow Buddhist flags flapping in the wind to a background of soft dharma music gives this space an energetic pulse. On the drive up, you'll wind past terraces of banana groves and tangles of jungle.

Meditation

You're on holiday so you probably won't be spending hours meditating, but you're in luck. Just before you head up the stairs to the plateau, you'll find the public seven-minute happiness meditation area, with a detailed photo guide for independent meditation.

Nearby: Chalong Bay Rum

About 8km east of Big Buddha, off Rte 4021 (look for zoo signs), is Phuket's only working distillery. **Chalong Bay Rum** (☎093 575 1119; www.chalongbay rum.com; 14/2 Mu 2, Soi Palai 2; tour 300B; ☺tours hourly 2-6pm; ℗) was launched by a young French couple who bonded over booze, particularly rum. Sip a mojito concocted with their delicious product on the 30-minute tour (book ahead).

พระใหญ่

www.mingmongkolphuket.com

off Rte 4021

admission free

☺6am-7pm

℗

☑ Top Tips

▶ As with all religious sites, dress conservatively. Women, especially, should cover up past the knee and over the shoulders. If needed, you'll be loaned a shawl.

▶ Don't miss the excellent viewpoint hidden in the rocks just off the main access stairs.

▶ From Big Buddha, head 14km northeast to explore the rich heritage of Phuket Town.

✗ Take a Break

About 450m below, open-air **Star Mountain & Sunset** (Big Buddha, off Rte 4021; mains 80-300B; ☺noon-6pm, hours vary) serves Thai staples alongside stellar views.

Explore

Ao Bang Thao

Ao Bang Thao's stunning, 8km-long white-sand beach is a journey into Phuket's psyche. The southern half is dotted with three-star bungalows; inland you'll find an old fishing village. Smack in the centre is the bizarre Laguna Phuket complex of five-star resorts. At the northern end, Mother Nature, thankfully, reasserts herself with a lonely stretch of powder-white sand and tropical blue sea.

The Region in a Day

☼ Ao Bang Thao is all about doing nothing, against a blissful beach backdrop. There are no real 'sights' to get you out of bed early here, so have a lie in and then amble down to **Hat Bang Thao** (p97) for a morning dip in the sea. Once you start getting peckish, pop just inland to **Cafe de Bangtao** (p98) for simple Thai and European staples, or stick with Thai and beachfront views at **Andaman Restaurant** (p99).

☼ Spend the afternoon stretching out on your rattan sun lounger at **Bliss Beach Club** (p98), being waited on hand and foot, sipping cocktails and exotic juices under casuarina trees, and deciding between swimming in the sea or the pool. For something to 'do', hunt down a good old Thai massage at **Thai Carnation** (p97).

☽ Treat yourself to a gourmet meal at hot new favourite **Bampot** (p97) or, on Mondays, catch jazz at **Siam Supper Club** (p98). Keep the fun going at stylish **Xana Beach Club** (p97) or drink into the night to a Rasta soundtrack at **Reggae Bar** (p99).

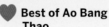 **Best of Ao Bang Thao**

Dining
Bliss Beach Club (p98)

Relaxing
Bliss Beach Club (p98)

Xana Beach Club (p97)

Thai Carnation (p97)

Getting There

🚕 **Taxi** Private taxis to/from the airport cost 700B. To/from Phuket's southern beaches costs about 900B.

Túk-túk Charters to/from Phuket Town cost around 400B.

Sŏrng·tăa·ou These passenger pick-up trucks run between Phuket Town's Th Ranong and Ao Bang Thao (25B) from 7am to 5pm.

For reviews see
Experiences   p97
Eating   p97
Drinking   p97

500 m
0.25 miles

N

Xana 3
Beach Club

Laguna
Phuket

Th Pasak-Koktanod

Thai
Carnation
Th Laguna 4

Soi Cherngtalay 16

Th Laguna

6   8 9
7   Th Bandon-
      Cherngtalay

Th Srisoonthorn

Ao Bang
Thao

Hat
Bang
Thao   13

Hat
Bang ⦿ 2
Thao
Bliss ⦿ 1
Beach
Club

Th Hat Bang Thao

Th Hat Bang Thao

CHERNGTALAY

Soi Bang Thao 2
Yopa

Th Hat Bang Thao

10
11

ANDAMAN
SEA

4030

4025

Experiences

Bliss Beach Club
BEACH CLUB

 Map p96, B3

s if Hat Bang Thao wasn't stunning
nough, Bliss offers the ultimate super-
wish Phuket beach experience. Mellow
nes beat in the background, guests
ounge around on the shady sea-facing
rrace and watching the kids splash
round the pool. Admission covers a
n lounger, a towel and use of the
cilities. (076 510150; www.blissbeach
ub.com; 202/88 Mu 2, Hat Bang Thao; day
ss 300B; 11am-late;)

at Bang Thao
BEACH

Map p96, B3

eautiful 8km-long Hat Bang Thao is
ne of the longest beaches on Phuket.
his dreamy slice of snow-white sand
ixes midrange bungalows (south
d), luxury resorts (in the middle) and
ot much else (north end).

ana Beach Club
BEACH CLUB

Map p96, C1

tering to a fashionable, mixed, fun-
ving crowd, Xana sits on a fabulous
ath of soft-white sand, halfway
ong gorgeous Hat Bang Thao. Come
r the polished red-on-white decor,
ised 35m pool, glitzy eight-person
banas, 'Sunday Fun Brunch', pound-
g international DJ house sets and
cked-out events (check Twitter
XanaBeachClub). (076 324101; www.
nabeachclub.com; 10 Mu 4, Hat Bang Thao;

day pass low/high season from 1000/1500B;
10am-midnight Sun-Fri, 10am-1am Sat)

Thai Carnation
SPA

4 Map p96, D2

Impressively professional yet wonderfully low-key, this fantastic-value spa
is a real find, with private massage
rooms, well-trained therapists and a
local vibe. It's 1.5km east (inland) from
Hat Bang Thao. (076 325565; www.
thai-carnation.com; 64 Th Laguna; massage
500-700B; 11am-10pm)

Yoga Republic
YOGA

5 Map p96, D4

A stylish, contemporary studio, complete with a health-kick juice bar, that
hosts an excellent line-up of drop-in
yoga sessions to suit all levels. It's on
Rte 4025, 2km east (inland) from Hat
Bang Thao. (076 324552; www.yoga
republic.co; 123/3-5 Mu 5, Th Srisoonthorn,
Bang Thao; class 550B; 9am-8pm)

Eating & Drinking

Bampot
INTERNATIONAL $$$

6 Map p96, D3

The latest fabulous arrival on Bang
Thao's food scene is suitably classy
with a modern, urban edge. Cool-blue
booths, dangling pans, black-topped
tables and white brick walls hung
with art set the scene for ambitious
Euro-inspired meals (lobster mac and
cheese, sea bass ceviche with pomelo)

straight from the open-plan kitchen. (☏093 586 9828; www.bampot.co; 19/1 Mu 1, Th Laguna; mains 500-600B; ⏰6pm-midnight Tue-Fri, noon-3pm & 6pm-midnight Sat & Sun)

Bliss Beach Club INTERNATIONAL $$$

Even if you don't commit to the Sunday party or a day indulging in these plush turquoise-and-orange-on-white surrounds, swing by Bliss (see 1 ◉ Map p96, B3) for a tasty lunch or dinner. The Thai-international menu of 13-inch wood-fired pizzas, roast pumpkin and quinoa salad, chicken satay, burgers and quesadillas is served on a beachside deck with gorgeous sea views. (☏076 510150; www.blissbeachclub.com; 202/88 Mu 2, Hat Bang Thao; mains 400-720B; ⏰11am-late; 🛜)

Pesto THAI, INTERNATIONAL $$

7 Map p96, E3

Mix a Paris-trained Thai chef with a tiny roadside shack and you've got a fantastic find for delicious, wallet-friendly Thai and international food. Try light pesto pasta, lobster lasagne and roast-pumpkin salad or stay local with *dôm yam gûng* (spicy-sour prawn soup), deep-fried turmeric fish of the day, and all your favourite curries. (☏082 423 0184; Th Bandon-Cherngtalay; mains 69-479B; ⏰11.30am-11pm Sun-Fri, 5-11pm Sat; 🍴)

Siam Supper Club INTERNATIONAL $$$

8 Map p96, E3

One of the swishest spots on Phuket to sip cocktails, listen to jazz and eat an excellent meal. The menu is predominantly international with gourmet pizzas, grilled goats' cheese and hearty mains such as barbecued Tasmanian salmon, plenty of pastas and truffle-honey roast chicken. Monday night jazz (8pm) is hugely popular; book ahead. (☏076 270936; www.siamsupperclub.com; 36-40 Th Laguna; mains 290-1250B; ⏰6pm-1am; 🍴)

Tatonka INTERNATIONAL $$$

9 Map p96, E3

Tatonka bills itself as the home of 'globetrotter cuisine', which owner-chef Harold Schwarz has developed by combining local products with cooking techniques learned in Europe, Colorado and Hawaii. The eclectic, tapas-style selection includes inventive vegetarian and seafood dishes and such delights as Peking duck pizza, green-curry pasta and eggplant 'cookies' with goats cheese. Book ahead in high season. (☏076 324349; 382/19 Mu 1, Th Laguna; dishes 180-790B; ⏰6-10pm Mon-Sat; 🍴)

Cafe de Bangtao INTERNATIONAL $$

10 Map p96, B4

A cute terracotta-tiled cafe with candle-lit tables, cane lanterns, friendly waitstaff and a tiki bar, at the southern end of Hat Bang Thao. Dishes range from all-day European breakfasts (pancakes, omelettes) and tasty, reasonably priced Thai dishes to pork tenderloin, pasta and pizza. (www.facebook.com/cafedebangtao; 69/19 Mu 3, Hat Bang Thao; mains 140-450B; ⏰8am-1am; 🛜)

Understand
Moo·ay tai

Moo·ay tai (Thai boxing; also spelled *muay Thai*) is Thailand's indigenous martial art and the nation's favourite sport. 'The art of eight limbs' captivates with its emphasis on close-quarters fighting. Fighters use knees, elbows, feet and fists to mimic weapons and inflict damage.

The story goes that in 1774, after Burma sacked Ayuthaya in 1767, the Burmese king held a seven-day, seven-night religious festival in honour of Lord Buddha. Overcome by an un-Buddhist impulse, he challenged Nai Khanom Tom, a Thai prisoner of war and a *moo·ay tai* expert, to fight a Burmese boxer. Nai Khanom Tom did a traditional *wai kroo* pre-fight dance (which loosens up the fighter and honours the teacher and, in this case, the Burmese king) before crushing his opponent. The baffled king made Nai Khanom Tom fight until he'd defeated nine Burmese champions in a row and won his freedom (plus two Burmese wives).

Originally *moo·ay tai* was taught in the military, but Buddhist monasteries inherited stewardship. International recognition and training for foreigners (both men and women) has soared in popularity in recent years, particularly on Phuket, where *moo·ay tai* camps flourish around Rawai.

---

ndaman Restaurant   THAI $$

 1 Map p96, B4

rt of the Andaman Bangtao Bay Re-ort, this simple seaside restaurant has laid-back castaway feel with bamboo nterns and driftwood furniture. Dine n decent-enough BBQ seafood and hai curries. (82/9 Mu 3, Hat Bang Thao; ains 195-295B; ☺8am-10pm; 🛜)

lok & Jo's   THAI, INTERNATIONAL $$

2 Map p96, A4

n a quiet road, 300m from the outhern end of the beach, sits this amshackle, ranch-feel sports bar and staurant serving an extensive mix of hai and international dishes. There's

fun *gà·teu·i* cabaret (ladyboys; also spelt *kàthoey*) and BBQ buffets on Sunday (500B), plus live music Tuesday to Sunday. (☑081 538 2110; www.facebook.com/Nok-Jos-Famous-Restaurant-Bang-tao-150777748318923; 37/1 Mu 3, Hat Bang Thao; mains 100-500B; ☺noon-late; 🛜)

Reggae Bar   BAR

 13 Map p96, B2

Stroll halfway down Hat Bang Thao to this friendly family-run beach bar, where Bob Marley soothes your soul. It's closed down, moved around and popped back up again as part of Phuket's recent beach clean-up operation, so ask locally for its latest location. (Hat Bang Thao; ☺9am-late)

Explore

Thalang & Around

Phuket's lush northeastern hemisphere is laced with temples, water-falls, singing gibbons and white-knuckle jungle zip lines. Unfolding around the Heroines Monument, 13km north of Phuket Town, untouristed Thalang conceals some worthwhile cultural attractions. Khao Phra Thaew Royal Wildlife & Forest Reserve, just north, makes for a fun day's adventure through Phuket's tropical rainforest.

The Region in a Day

Arrive early to see **Wat Phra Thong** (p104) in the morning sun, before diving into **Khao Phra Thaew Royal Wildlife & Forest Reserve** (p103) to learn about the island's gibbons at the **Phuket Gibbon Rehabilitation Project** (p103). Ask about guided hikes at the park's entrance, or take yourself off along a jungle-fringed path for a dip at **Nam Tok Bang Pae** (p104). After all the action, you'll be starving, so drop in at **Monkeypod** (p105) for an espresso and a light lunch. If you fancy freshly caught seafood instead, head over to mangrove-shaded **Bang Rong Seafood** (p105).

Spend the afternoon uncovering fascinating historical facts at the dusty but excellent **Thalang National Museum** (p104), then rouse yourself with an adrenaline hit ziplining through the jungle at **Cable Jungle Adventures** (p105).

Things go pretty quiet around Thalang once the sun goes down. Make your way over to Laem amu and cool blue **Breeze Restaurant** (p105) – one of Phuket's top eateries – for a stylish European-fusion dinner with never-ending views of turquoise water and jungle-coated hills.

 Best of Thalang

For Kids
Khao Phra Thaew Royal Wildlife & Forest Reserve (p103)

Phuket Gibbon Rehabilitation Project (p103)

Nam Tok Bang Pae (p104)

Cultural Experiences
Thalang National Museum (p104)

Wat Phra Thong (p104)

Dining
Breeze Restaurant (p105)

Monkeypod (p105)

Bang Rong Seafood (p105)

Getting There

Sŏrng·tǎa·ou These (passenger pick-up trucks) run four times daily between Phuket Town and Tha Bang Rong (50B) from 8.30am to 4pm.

Taxi From Tha Bang Rong to Phuket's west-coast resort areas, taxis cost 600B to 800B.

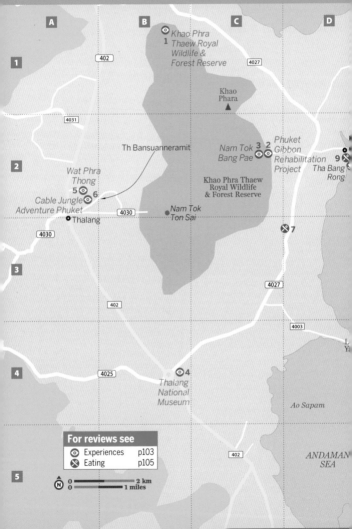

Khao Phra
Thaew Royal
Wildlife &
Forest Reserve

1

402

4027

Khao
Phara

4031

Th Bansuanneramit

Nam Tok
Bang Pae

Phuket
Gibbon
Rehabilitation
Project

9

Tha Bang
Rong

Wat Phra
Thong

Khao Phra Thaew
Royal Wildlife
& Forest Reserve

Cable Jungle
Adventure Phuket

4030

Nam Tok
Ton Sai

Thalang

4030

7

4027

4003

402

4025

4

Thalang
National
Museum

Ao Sapam

ANDAMAN
SEA

For reviews see

⊙ Experiences p103
⊗ Eating p105

N 0 ————————— 2 km
   0 ————————— 1 miles

Nam Tok Bang Pae (p104)

Experiences

Khao Phra Thaew Royal Wildlife & Forest Reserve

WILDLIFE RESERVE

1 ◎ Map p102, B1

On the north half of the island, this reserve protects 23 sq km of evergreen monsoon forest. Because of its royal status, it's better protected than the average national park in Thailand. Tigers, Malayan sun bears, rhinos and elephants once roamed the forest here, but nowadays resident animals are limited to humans, wild boars, monkeys, slow loris, langurs, gibbons, civets, flying foxes, cobras, pythons, squirrels and other smaller creatures. (อุทยาน สัตว์ป่าเขาพระแทว; off Rte 4027 & Hwy 402; adult/child 200/100B)

Phuket Gibbon Rehabilitation Project

WILDLIFE RESERVE

2 ◎ Map p102, C2

Financed by donations (1800B cares for a gibbon for a year), this tiny sanctuary adopts gibbons that have been kept in captivity in the hope that they can be reintroduced to the wild. Swing by around 9am to hear the gibbons' morning song. You can't get too close, which may disappoint kids, but the volunteer work done here is outstanding. (โครงการคืนชะนีสู่ป่า; ☏076 260492; www. gibbonproject.org; off Rte 4027; admission by donation; ⊙9am-4.30pm, to 3pm Thu; Ⓟ)

Nam Tok Bang Pae

WATERFALL

3 ◎ Map p102, C2

The waterfall is a 300m walk up a jungled earth-and-concrete path from the gibbon rehab centre, and you can hear the gibbons' haunting songs all the way. During the dry season, the waterfall isn't exactly spectacular, but there are swimming holes deep enough for daring jumps. The falls are best seen in the rainy season between June and November. (off Rte 4027; adult/child 200/100B)

Thalang National Museum

MUSEUM

4 ◎ Map p102, B4

This excellent museum chronicles Phuket's history, from prehistoric Andaman inhabitants to the tin-mining era, with Thai and English displays. It traces southern Thailand's varied ethnicities and dialects, and recounts the legend of the 'two heroines' (immortalised on the nearby Heroines Monument). The prize entrance-hall artefact is a 2.3m-tall 9th-century stone statue of Vishnu, found in Takua Pa in the early 20th century. (พิพิธภัณฑสถานแห่งชาติถลาง; ☎076 379895; Th Srisoonthorn/ Rte 4027; admission 100B; ⊙9am-4pm Wed-Sun; Ⓟ)

Wat Phra Thong

BUDDHIST TEMPLE

5 ◎ Map p102, A2

About 7km north of the Heroines Monument, Phuket's 'Temple of the Golden Buddha' is half buried, so only the head and shoulders are visible. According to legend, those who have tried to excavate the image have

Understand
Thalang's Heroines

The untimely death of Thalang's governor in 1785 left Phuket in a vulnerable position as the 144,000-strong fleet of invading Burmese troops set upon the island with no one to take charge. Left with no choice the governor's wife, Lady Chan, and her sister, Lady Mook, assembled the local forces and prepared for battle. To fool the Burmese army the sisters called upon the residents of Phuket, including women, to dress up as soldiers so their military 'manpower' would seem invincible to Burmese scouts.

It proved a masterstroke and the Burmese rapidly retreated on 13 March 1785. The sisters became heroines and King Rama I bestowed upon them the respective honorary titles of Thao Thepkasattri and Thao Sri Sunthorn. Today they stand immortalised side by side, swords in hand, at Thalang's Heroines Monument on Hwy 402, 13km north of Phuket Town. The sisters remain highly revered and a major festival is held annually on 13 March to commemorate their victory, with re-enactments by hundreds of performers.

become very ill or encountered serious accidents. The temple is particularly revered by Thai-Chinese, who believe the image hails from China. During Chinese New Year, pilgrims descend from Phang-Nga, Takua Pa and Krabi. Also here are a crematorium and a historical museum. (วัดพระทอง; off Hwy 402; admission free; ⊙dawn-dusk; [P])

Cable Jungle Adventure Phuket ADVENTURE SPORTS

6 Map p102, A2

Tucked into the hills behind a quilt of pineapple fields, rubber plantations and mango groves is this maze of zip lines linking ancient ficus trees. The zips range from 6m to 50m above the ground and the longest run is 300m long. Closed-toe shoes are a must. Staff will pick you up from your hotel. (☏081 977 4904; www.cablejunglephuket.com; 232/17 Mu 8, Th Bansuanneramit; per person 2150B; ⊙9am-5pm)

Eating

Monkeypod CAFE $$

7 Map p102, D3

A striking minimalist-white creation with floor-to-ceiling windows and a leafy outlook, this modern family-run cafe is a welcome surprise along Rte 4027 to Khao Phra Thaew Royal Wildlife & Forest Reserve. The espresso coffee is exceptional. Smoothies and cafe food are delicious too, with reasonably priced salads, pastas,

wraps and Phuketian classics. It's 6km northeast of the Heroines Monument. (www.facebook.com/MonkeypodCoffeehouse; cnr Th Lum Sai & Rte 4027; mains 140-200B; ⊙10am-8.30pm; 🛜)

Breeze Restaurant INTERNATIONAL $$$

8 Map p102, D4

Classy yet understated, one of Phuket's finest restaurants sits in glorious hilltop, sea-surrounded seclusion, 20km northeast of Phuket Town. Blue beanbags overlook pool and sea from the pillared open-walled dining hall. Weekly-changing menus triumph with divine, inventive European-style dishes infused with local produce. Pair with classic cocktails given a Thai twist. Book for Sunday brunch (1930B). (☏081 271 2320; www.breezecapeyamu.com; Laem Yamu; mains 275-750B; ⊙noon-10pm Wed-Sat, to 4pm Sun; 🛜)

Bang Rong Seafood THAI, SEAFOOD $

9 Map p102, D2

This rustic fish-farm-turned-restaurant sits on a floating pier amid the mangroves, accessed via a wooden boardwalk 750m east off Rte 4027. It does red and white snapper, crab and mussels, and plucks your catch after you order (so you know it's fresh). You can have everything steamed, fried, grilled, boiled or baked, but this is a Muslim enterprise so there's no beer. (☏093 737 9264, 081 370 3401; Tha Bang Rong, off Rte 4027; dishes 120-300B; ⊙9.45am-6pm)

Explore

Northern Beaches

Phuket's northwest coast is one of its sweetest slices. Within 15 minutes of the airport lie some of the island's dreamiest and least developed beaches: magnificent Hat Mai Khao, fun-loving Hat Nai Yang and easy-going Hat Nai Thon, protected as Sirinat National Park. If you're chasing what remains of Phuket's beach seclusion and tranquility, where nature and tourism still co-exist, this is it.

The Region in a Day

Once you've rolled out of bed, grab a coffee and croissant at **Bread & Butter** (p111) before whizzing off to play with furry friends at **Soi Dog** (p109) and touring the foundation's facilities. Laze away the rest of the morning amid lotus ponds at **Bua Luang Spa** (p110). Once lunchtime rolls around, pull up a plastic chair for tasty Thai at **Mr Kobi** (p111) or tuck into fresh seafood with a side of sea glimpses at **Coconut Tree** (p111).

Set aside the afternoon for lounging on the sand of whichever beach takes your fancy. If you get restless, enjoy a lengthy stroll along **Hat Mai Khao** (p109) or fly across the waves with a kitesurfing class at **Kite Zone** (p109). Otherwise, if you're visiting with kids, the waterslide maze at **Splash Jungle** (p110) will keep everyone entertained.

As the sun goes down, stroll along heavenly **Hat Nai Thon** (p109) to swish clifftop **Elements** (p111), where classy Thai fare and sensational Andaman vistas are guaranteed, or go for laid-back boutique international dining at **Terrace Grill** (p111).

Best of the Northern Beaches

Beaches

Hat Nai Thon (p109)

Hat Nai Yang (p109)

Hat Mai Khao (p109)

Spas & Massages

Bua Luang Spa (p110)

Sala Spa (p110)

Coqoon Spa (p110)

Getting There

🚗 **Taxi** Private taxi to/from the airport costs 200B. To/from Patong is about 900B.

Túk-túk A túk-túk charter from Phuket Town costs 550B.

A   B   C   D

Bua Luang Spa ◉ 7   402

1

Sala Spa ◉ 8

Hat Mai Khao ◉ 4

402

Yacht Haven Phuket Marina

13 ◉ *Asia Marine*

Ao Tha Maphrao

Hat Mai Khao

2

ANDAMAN SEA

5 ◉ *Soi Dog*

Th Ban Mai Khao

Splash Jungle ◉ 11

Phuket International Airport   4031

3

1 ◉ Sirinat National Park

14 ⊗

● Ban Sakhu

402

Kiteboarding Asia 9 ⊗

Kite Zone 6 ◉

Hat Nai Yang 3 ◉ ⊗ 15

Hat Nai Yang ◉ 10 *Coqoon Spa*

4026   4027

Khao Phra Th Royal Wildlife Forest Rese

4

16 ⊗

Ao Nai Thon

12 ◉ *Waree Spa*

2 ◉ *Hat Nai Thon*

Hat Nai Thon ◉ ⊗ 17

Th Hat Nai Thon

402

4031

5

Hat Layan ◉

For reviews see

◉ Experiences   p109
⊗ Eating   p111

N

0   2 km
0   1 miles

Experiences

Sirinat National Park
NATIONAL PARK

1 Map p108, B3

Comprising the exceptional beaches of Nai Thon, Nai Yang and Mai Khao, as well as the former Nai Yang National Park and Mai Khao wildlife reserve, Sirinat National Park encompasses 22 sq km of coastal land, plus 68 sq km of sea, stretching from just beyond the northern end of Ao Bang Thao to the northernmost tip of the island. Sea turtles patrol the reef and lay eggs on Hat Mai Khao. Park headquarters is at the northern end of Hat Nai Yang. (อุทยานแห่งชาติสิรินาต; ☎076 327152, 076 328226; www.dnp.go.th; adult/child 200/100B; ⊙8.30am-4pm)

Hat Nai Thon
BEACH

2 Map p108, A5

If you're after a lovely arc of fine golden sand, away from Phuket's busy buzz, come to west-coast Hat Nai Thon, 7km south of the airport. Swimming is good (except at the height of the monsoon), and there's coral near the headlands at either end of the bay. Many beach restaurants here were demolished by the island clean-up.

Hat Nai Yang
BEACH

3 Map p108, B4

Hat Nai Yang's bay, 3km south of the airport, is sheltered by a reef that slopes 20m below the surface – which means good snorkelling in high season and fantastic surfing and kite-surfing during the monsoon. Behind is a long strip of seafood restaurants, hotels and mellow bars. It's delightfully rough around the edges.

Hat Mai Khao
BEACH

4 Map p108, B1

Phuket's longest beach is a beautiful, secluded 10km stretch extending from just south of the airport to the island's northernmost point. Except on weekends and holidays, you may have it to yourself. Sea turtles lay eggs here between November and February. There's a strong year-round undertow.

Soi Dog
VOLUNTEERING

5 Map p108, B2

This non-profit foundation protects 50 cats and 450 dogs (many rescued from the illegal dog-meat trade), focusing on sterilisation, re-homing and animal welfare awareness. Visitors can play with the animals, or become a dog-walking or long-term volunteer. (☎081 788 4222; www.soidog.org; 167/9 Mu 4, Soi Mai Khao 10; admission by donation; ⊙9am-noon & 1-3.30pm Mon-Fri, tours 9.30am, 11am & 1.30pm)

Kite Zone
KITESURFING

6 Map p108, B4

Highly professional operator that runs on Nai Yang during the monsoon season and has a year-round branch in Rawai. Also rents kit (per hour/day

1200/3500B) and organises stand-up paddle trips (from 700B). (☎083 395 2005; www.kitesurfthailand.com; Hat Nai Yang; 1hr lesson 1100B, 3-day course 10,000-15,000B; ☻May–late-Oct)

Bua Luang Spa   SPA

7 ◎ Map p108, B1

Escape into a tranquil, elegant oasis of lotus-filled ponds and timber board-walks with exotic treatments including avocado scrubs, lavender salt glow, Ayurvedic head massages and full-day rituals (from 6000B). (☎076 336 1000; www.phuket.anantara.com; Anantara Phuket, 888 Mu 3, Hat Mai Khao; treatment 3500-5900B; ☻10am-10pm)

Sala Spa   SPA

8 ◎ Map p108, B1

Enjoy your aromatherapy massage or soothing water-lily body wrap at this elegant and sexy, yet not full of itself, spa resort. Choose to indulge in your own peaceful private tub in a pebbled courtyard or enjoy a beachfront massage. It's the kind of place that makes everyone feel fabulous. (☎076 338888; www.salaphuket.com; Sala Phuket, 333 Mu 3, Hat Mai Khao; treatment 2200-4100B; ☻10am-10pm)

Kiteboarding Asia   KITESURFING

9 ◎ Map p108, B3

A large-scale, professional kitesurfing operator with branches across Thailand. It's based on Hat Nai Yang during the monsoon, but also offer

lessons off Rawai's Hat Friendship from November to March. (☎081 591 4594; www.kiteboardingasia.com; Hat Nai Yang; 1hr lesson 1300B, 3-day course 11,000B; ☻Apr-Oct)

Coqoon Spa   SPA

10 ◎ Map p108, B4

Set in a 277-room megaresort that doubles as a monument to Phuket's tin-mining past – vices, scales and other mining tools detail the decor – this is a fantastic, unique spa where treatments rooms are backed by lush gardens. Treatments include purple frangipani scrubs, bamboo charcoal wraps and detoxes in a suspended 'nest' suite. (☎076 327006; www.indigo-pearl.com; Indigo Pearl, 116 Mu 1, Hat Nai Yang; treatment 2200-7000B; ☻9am-8pm)

Splash Jungle   WATER PARK

11 ◎ Map p108, B3

Within eyeshot of Phuket airport, this massive water park has a wave pool, a kids' pool with water cannons, 12 multicoloured twisting water slides for all ages, a 'superbowl' slide and...a bar. Book ahead and the price will include pick-up from your resort. (☎076 372111; www.splashjunglewaterpark.com; 65 Mu 4, Soi 4, Mai Khao; adult/5-12yr/under 5yr 1295/650B/free; ☻10am-6pm)

Waree Spa   SPA

12 ◎ Map p108, A5

This sweet, family-owned spa has basic but tasteful environs, a proper

Scandinavian sauna (high season only) and a variety of massage classics on the menu. (☏084 648 2192; 24 Mu 4, Th Hat Nai Thon; massage 400-700B; ☺9am-9pm)

Asia Marine BOATING

13 Map p108, C1

One of Phuket's first yacht charters and with a diverse Andaman fleet, Asia Marine has a boat for everyone, from sleek fibreglass catamarans to wooden junks. High-season bareboat charters start at 143,000B. (☏076 206653; www.asia-marine.net; Phuket Yacht Haven Marina, 141/2 Mu 2, Laem Phrao)

Eating

Terrace Grill THAI, INTERNATIONAL $$

14 Map p108, B3

Swing by this beautiful upscale boutique resort for tasty Thai and international fare in a classy restaurant overlooking a lovely pool and a chill-out bar strewn with beanbags. It's particularly hot on meaty treats but packs in plenty of pastas, sandwiches, *pàt tai* and indulgent desserts too. (☏076 372300; www.dewaphuketresort.com; Dewa, 65 Mu 1, Hat Nai Yang; mains 250-440B; ☺6.30am-10.30pm; 🛜)

Mr Kobi THAI $$

15 Map p108, B4

The sign says, 'Broken English spoken here perfect', but the ever-popular

Mr Kobi speaks English very well. Tuck into inexpensive Thai faves in refreshingly scruffy surrounds. One wall is dedicated to telling the story of the 2004 tsunami. (Hat Nai Yang; mains 150-200B; ☺10am-10pm)

Elements THAI $$$

16 Map p108, A4

Perched high on the cliffs at the northern end of the beach, Nai Thon's sleekest resort offers sophisticated Thai food in a swish, spacious indoor-outdoor dining room with beautiful views across the bay. Lunch sees burgers and sandwiches thrown into the mix, and on Fridays they fire up a seafood BBQ (per person 1900B). (☏076 303299; www.pullmanphuketarcadia.com; Pullman, 22/2 Mu 4, Hat Nai Thon; mains 320-1100B; ☺6.30-11pm)

Bread & Butter CAFE $$

Pocketed away in the sultry Dewa resort (see 14 Map p108, B3), across the road from Hat Nai Yang, this tiny, modern orange-walled cafe is a decent spot to enjoy your morning espresso or green tea plus homemade classic pies, freshly baked bread, sandwiches, quiches, pizzas and bagels and sweet treats. (☏076 372300; Dewa, 65 Mu 1, Hat Nai Yang; dishes 150-250B; ☺7am-7pm)

Coconut Tree THAI $

17 Map p108, A5

This friendly relaxed food spot towards the south end of Hat Nai Thon rustles up quality fresh seafood dishes

Understand

The Marine Enviroment

Thailand's coral reef system, including the Andaman Coast from Ranong to northern Phuket and the Surin and Similan Islands, is one of the world's most diverse. Some 900 species of coral reef fish, endangered marine turtles and other rare creatures, such as whale sharks and giant manta rays, inhabit this coastline.

Environmental Issues

The 2004 Boxing Day tsunami caused high-impact damage to about 13% of the Andaman's coral reefs. However, the damage from the tsunami turned out to be much less extensive than initially thought and relatively minor compared to the relentless environmental degradation that accompanies an industrialised society.

Estimates indicate that 25% of Thailand's coral reefs have died as a result of industrial pollution and that the annual loss of healthy reefs will continue at a rapid rate. Even around dive-central Phuket, dead coral reefs have become noticeably more visible. The biggest threat to corals is sedimentation from coastal development (new hotels, roads, houses, businesses and industrial parks), which stunts coral growth.

Other increasingly common issues include pollution from anchored tour boats or other marine activities, rubbish and sewage dumped straight into the sea, agricultural and industrial run-off, over-fishing, destructive diving tourism, unmonitored tourist numbers and damage from boats anchoring directly on coral reefs. In recent years, rising sea temperatures have caused serious coral bleaching.

Responsible Travel

It's hard to ignore the rubbish on Phuket's beaches these days, particularly in high season, though things have been improving since the Phuket beach clean-up operation kicked off in 2014 (p67). Phuket generates an average of 729 tonnes of rubbish each day. Do your bit by, firstly, throwing your rubbish in the bin and, secondly, picking up other debris whenever you can.

When swimming, diving or snorkelling, do not touch or walk on coral, monitor your movements so you avoid accidentally sweeping into coral, and do not harass marine life.

Hawksbill sea turtle

such as stir-fried crab with black pepper, and tiger prawns cooked in everything from yellow curry to bitter ginger, on a rustic semi-open veranda with a few pot plants. The Andaman sparkles beyond soaring palms and casuarinas. (📞098 364 6366; Th Hat Nai Thon, Hat Nai Thon; mains 80-150B; ⏰11am-11pm; 🛜)

Phen's Restaurant THAI, SEAFOOD $$

Cream-coated umbrellas, turquoise-on-white tablecloths and attentive staff make Phen's a smartish, popular beachside choice (see 9 ⊙ Map p108, B3). It's one of few spots where you can still dine with sand between your toes. Expect token international dishes (burgers, sandwiches, spaghetti)

balanced out by masses of barbecued fresh seafood (lemon-fried crab, red-curry snapper, chilli-smoked shrimp), veg-laden stir fries, hot Thai soups and delightful tropical juices. (📞081 895 9489; www.facebook.com/Phens Restaurant; Hat Nai Yang; mains 100-300B; ⏰9.30am-10.30pm; 🛜)

Tien Seng THAI $

Cheap and tasty Thai faves and decent international breakfasts are yours at this humble, fairy-lit roadside eatery at the southern end of Hat Nai Thon (see 17 ❌ Map p108, A5). Tien Seng fires up the fish grill at night. (📞084 948 1826; 28 Th Hat Nai Thon, Hat Nai Thon; mains 60-250B; ⏰9am-9.30pm)

Top Experiences
Day-Trippin' Ko Phi-Phi

Getting There

Ko Phi-Phi is 47km southeast of Phuket.

⚓ Boats leave Phuket's Tha Rassada at 9am, 11am and 3pm, returning at 9am, 2pm, 2.30pm and 3.30pm (250B to 300B, two hours).

Curvy bays, bleach-blonde beaches, bodacious jungles and long-tails puttering between craggy cliffs that rise from vivid turquoise waters. The insanely pretty islands of Ko Phi-Phi Don and Ko Phi-Phi Leh turn tropical-island clichés into a stunning reality. Boat over to Phi-Phi Leh to retrace Leo DiCaprio's steps in *The Beach*, dive deep into the blue, hike up to the glorious viewpoint or just kick back for the day on any of the soft white sands sprinkled around.

Maya Bay, Ko Phi-Phi

Don't Miss

Diving

Phi-Phi's crystalline waters and abundant marine life make for top-notch scuba diving. Popular dive sites include **King Cruiser Wreck**, 12m underwater; **Anemone Reef**, teeming with clownfish; **Hin Bida Phi-Phi**, a submerged pinnacle; **Ko Bida Nok**, attracting leopard sharks; and new **Kledkaeo Wreck**. Join **Adventure Club** (📱081 895 334; www.diving-in-thailand.net; Ton Sai Village; 2 dives 2500B, Open Water certification 13,800B; ⊗8am-10pm) for two-dive trips.

Snorkelling

On Phi-Phi Don, there's good snorkelling along western Ko Nok (near Ao Ton Sai) and eastern Ko Nai, and off **Hat Yao** (Long Beach). **Ko Mai Phai** (Bamboo Island), 6km north of Phi-Phi Don, is a popular shallow snorkelling spot frequented by small sharks. Snorkelling trips cost 700B to 1500B.

Phi-Phi Viewpoint

The steep, strenuous climb to **Phi-Phi Viewpoint** (จุดชมวิวเกาะพีพีดอน; admission 30B) is a rewarding 20- to 30-minute hike up hundreds of steps and narrow twisting paths from northeast Ton Sai Village. The views from the top are exquisite: Phi-Phi's lush mountain butterfly brilliance in full bloom.

Ko Phi-Phi Leh

Ever since Alex Garland's cult classic *The Beach* became a film here, rugged Phi-Phi Leh has been something of a pilgrimage site, especially beautiful **Ao Maya** (Maya Bay; adult/child 400/200B). Visit aboard one of the outrageously popular half-day tours from Phi-Phi Don (from 900B) or by chartering a long-tail (700B to 800B).

Top Experiences
Rock Climbing in Railay, Krabi

Getting There

Railay is 50km east of Phuket.

⚓ Year-round ferries run from Phuket's Tha Rassada to Railay (700B, 2¼ hours) at 8.30am, returning at 3.15pm. Reduced services May to October.

Surrounded by fairy-tale limestone crags jutting out high above emerald waters and pure-white beaches, Krabi's Railay peninsula is the ultimate jungle gym for rock-climbing fanatics. With over 700 bolted routes, ranging from beginner to challenging advanced climbs, Railay is one of the top rock-climbing destinations in the world. And after scaling the limestone, hit those glorious turquoise waters, soak up the chilled-out Thai-Rasta vibe or pop over to Ao Nang, a quick long-tail ride northwest around the corner.

Don't Miss

Climbs

Most climbers start off at **Muay Thai Wall** and **One, Two, Three Wall**, on southern Hat Railay East, which have at least 40 routes graded from 5 to 8b on the French system. The mighty **Thailand Wall**, on southern Hat Railay West, offers some of the most challenging climbs. Other top climbs include **Hidden World**, **Wee's Present Wall**, **Diamond Cave** and **Ao Nang Tower**.

Climbing Schools

Basecamp Tonsai (☎081 149 9745; www.tonsaibasecamp.com; Hat Ton Sai; half/full day 800/1500B, 3-day course 6000B; ☺8am-5pm & 7-9pm) is arguably Railay's most professional climbing outfit. Longstanding **King Climbers** (☎081 797 8923; www.railay.com; Walking St; half/full day 1000/1800B, 3-day course 5000B; ☺8.30am-9pm Mon-Fri, to 6pm Sat & Sun) is also reputable.

Tham Phra Nang

Full of colourful wooden phalluses, **Tham Phra Nang** (ถ้ำพระนาง, Princess Cave; Hat Tham Phra Nang) is an important local shrine. Fishers (Muslim and Buddhist) make these offerings in the hope that the inhabiting spirit of a drowned Indian princess will provide a good catch. According to legend, a royal barge carrying the princess foundered here in a storm during the 3rd century BC.

Sa Phra Nang

Halfway along the trail linking Hat Railay East to Hat Tham Phra Nang, a short, steep 'path' (with climbing ropes) leads up a jungle-cloaked cliff wall then down to this little-visited hidden **lagoon** (Holy Princess Pool). Fork left at the summit to reach a dramatic cliff-side **viewpoint**.

☑ Top Tips

▶ Railay is only accessible by long-tail from nearby Ao Nang, Ao Nam Mao or Krabi (or by ferry from further afield).

▶ Tham Phra Nang is best visited in the early morning to avoid the day-tripping afternoon rush.

▶ Boat over to Ao Nang (100B, 15 minutes) for a livelier tourist-dominated scene.

✗ Take a Break

Once you're done tackling the rocks, refuel with spicy, affordable Thai favourites at local-style **Mangrove Restaurant** (Walking St; dishes 80-150B; ☺9am-10pm; ☎), or classy Mediterranean fare half-inside a cave at the **Grotto** (Hat Phra Nang; mains 460-820B; ☺noon-10pm).

Top Experiences
Hidden Hôrng of Ao Phang-Nga

Getting There

🚢 Best option: day trip with a Phuket-based operator (from 3000B).

🚌 Catch a bus from Phuket to Phang-Nga (85B, 2½ hours) and charter boats from Tha Dan, 9km south.

Between turquoise bays peppered with craggy limestone towers, brilliant-white beaches and tumble-down fishing villages, Ao Phang-Nga is one of the Andaman's most spectacular landscapes. The bay may be swarming with tourists in motorboats year-round, but, once you start navigating its majestic scenery, awe descends upon your suddenly silent group. With just the gentle lull of your kayak paddle in the water, sit back and enjoy the tranquil confines of its famous *hôrng* (semi-submerged island lagoons).

Ko Khao Phing Kan (James Bond Island)

Don't Miss

Ao Phang-Nga National Park

Established in 1981, 400-sq-km Ao Phang-Nga National Park is famous for its classic karst scenery, created by mainland fault movements pushing massive limestone blocks into geometric patterns. These blocks extended southward into Ao Phang-Nga, forming 42 islands dominated by huge vertical cliffs. The bay itself is composed of large and small tidal channels, which run north to south through vast mangroves.

Hôrng by Starlight

Slip through pitch-black bat caves into hidden lagoons protected by limestone cliffs that tower up from the sea. Along the way you'll be accompanied by sea eagles, and you may spot monkeys, pythons and monitor lizards, making the experience all the more exotic. Reputable and ecologically sensitive, **John Gray's Seacanoe** (p30) was the first kayak outfitter in the bay. The Hong by Starlight trip dodges the crowds, involves sunset paddling and will introduce you to Ao Phang-Nga's famed after-dark bioluminescence.

The Islands

Ao Phang-Nga National Park's biggest tourist drawcard is **Ko Khao Phing Kan** (เกาะเขาพิงกัน, James Bond Island). Once used as a location setting for *The Man with the Golden Gun*, today the island is packed with vendors hawking coral and shells that should have stayed in the sea. A stilted Muslim village clings to **Ko Panyi** (เกาะปันหยี), where you can spend the night for a more peaceful experience.

อุทยานแห่งชาติอ่าวพังงา

☏ 076 481188

www.dnp.go.th

adult/child 300/100B

🕗 8am-4pm

☑ Top Tips

▶ Explore in the early morning or stay out for the evening to sidestep the crowds.

▶ It's easiest to join a sea-canoeing trip as a day tour from Phuket.

▶ Stay overnight on Ko Panyi to soak up the stunning scenery without interruptions.

▶ Pack your hat, swimsuit, sunnies and sunscreen.

✗ Take a Break

Most tours include lunch. Otherwise, dine at the simple, rustic riverside **national park restaurant** (dishes 60B) near Tha Dan or head 9km north to Phang-Nga's street stalls and night market.

Top Experiences
Diving in the Similan Islands

Getting There

🚢 Day/overnight tours (from 2900/5000B), two-dive day trips (from 5000B) and multi-day live-aboards (from 16,000B to 19,000B) from Phuket or Khao Lak are best for Similans access.

Famous among divers the world over, the beautiful 70-sq-km Similan Islands Marine National Park is Thailand's premier dive spot. Its smooth granite islands are as impressive above the bright-aqua water as below, topped with rainforest, edged with blindingly white beaches, fringed by kaleidoscopic coral reefs and teeming with exotic wildlife. Underwater lie dramatic gorges and boulder swim-throughs. The archipelago comprises 11 idyllic islands; while each is named, most are known by numbers.

Don't Miss

Going Underwater

The Similans offer diving for all levels, at depths from 2m to 30m. There are rock reefs at **Ko Hin Pousar** (Island 7) and dive-throughs at **Hin Pousar** (Elephant Head Rock), with marine life ranging from tiny plume worms and soft corals to schooling fish, manta rays and rare whale sharks. **Ko Bon** and **Ko Tachai**, largely unscathed by coral bleaching, are some of the better diving and snorkeling areas. There are dive sites at each of the six islands north of **Ko Miang**.

Hiking

Life isn't all below water here. A small beach track leads 400m east from Ko Miang's visitors centre to a tiny snorkelling bay. Detouring from this track, the **Viewpoint Trail**, about 500m (30 minutes) of steep scrambling, has panoramic vistas from the top. A 500m (20-minute) forest walk west from the visitors centre leads to west-facing granite platform **Sunset Point**. On **Ko Similan** (Island 8), there's a 2.5km forest hike to a **viewpoint**, and a shorter, steep scramble off the north-coast beach to **Sail Rock** (Balance Rock).

Wildlife

The forest around Ko Miang's visitors centre has great wildlife. The fabulous Nicobar pigeon, with its wild mane of grey-green feathers, is common here. Endemic to the islands of the Andaman Sea, it's one of 39 bird species in the park. Hairy-legged land crabs and fruit bats (flying foxes) are relatively easy to spot in the forest, as are flying squirrels.

อุทยานแห่งชาติหมู่เกาะสิมิลัน

☎ 076 453272

www.dnp.go.th

adult/child 500/300B

⊙ mid-Oct–mid-May

☑ Top Tips

▶ The Similans close mid-May to mid-October.

▶ Diving is always good, but February to April has top visibility.

▶ Stay overnight to experience the park's beauty without day-tripping chaos.

▶ Unmonitored tourism is damaging the park's environment. Tread lightly; don't feed fish.

▶ The park visitors centre and facilities are on north-coast Ko Miang (Island 4).

✕ Take a Break

A park **restaurant** (Ko Miang; dishes 120-150B, lunch buffet 230B; ⊙7.30am-8.30pm) serves simple Thai meals, but tours usually include food.

The Best of
Phuket

Vegetarian Festival (p33)
ASHIT DESA / GETTY IMAGES ©

Best Walks
Phuket Town's Architectural Legacies

🏃 The Walk

On an island that reels in six million beach-goers yearly, it's easy to overlook wonderful Phuket Town, with its lack of white sands, blue waters and fiery sunsets. But Phuket Town offers a rare insight into the island's history and this walk through its core Old Town will lead you past the mid-19th-century architectural legacies, grand mansions and narrow shophouses of the Baba (also known as Peranakan or Straits-Chinese) people.

Start Memory at On On Hotel

Finish Phuket Thaihua Museum

Length 2km; two hours

🍴 Take a Break

There are some sensational local-flavoured food stops tucked into Sino-Portuguese shophouses along Th Thalang, including Kopitiam by Wilai (p25), which serves fantastic Phuket soul food.

LYNN GAIL / GETTY IMAGES ©

Phuket Thaihua Museum

❶ Memory at On On Hotel

Start with the smartly revamped **Memory at On On Hotel**. Phuket's first hotel sprawls behind its gleaming-white Sino-Portuguese facade to terracotta-tiled patios mosaic-floored halls and imposing wooden staircases.

❷ Standard Chartered Bank

Wander east to the recently restored **Standard Chartered Bank** (p28) in classic Sino-Portuguese style. Thailand's first local bank, it's now an erratically open museum showcasing Phuket's Baba history.

❸ Police Station

Opposite is the **Thai police building**, with an early 1990s unique four-storey clock tower and traditional police-cap roof. The clock-tower face stood blank for 50 years until budget allowed a clock.

❹ Philatetic Museum

Head east along Th Phang-Nga, noting

ateries in beautiful hophouses. Turn north left) onto Th Montri and you'll spot the old post office, a magnificent (if flaking) example of Sino-Portuguese architecture now housing the **Phuket Philatelic Museum** (p28).

5 Soi Romanee

Continue north along Th Montri and turn west left) down historical Th Thalang, packed with converted shophouses. Head right onto gorgeous **Soi Romanee**, where vividly restored Sino-Portuguese shop-

houses turned boutique hotels shimmer under Chinese paper lanterns.

6 Phra Phitak Chyn Pracha Mansion

Turn west (left) to the end of Th Dibuk then head south (left) along Th Satun to Th Krabi. Wander into the gardens on the corner. The early-20th-century **Phra Phitak Chyn Pracha Mansion** here has been immaculately restored as one of Phuket's finest restaurants and cooking schools, **Blue Elephant** (p31).

7 Chyn Pracha House

Beside Blue Elephant, a path leads to **Chyn Pracha House** (p27), built in 1903 on tin-mining wealth. It's now a private home/museum.

8 Phuket Thaihua Museum

Head back east to **Phuket Thaihua Museum** (p27). Dating from 1934, this was the oldest Chinese school in Thailand and exhibits European-Sino-Thai architectural styles and local-life displays.

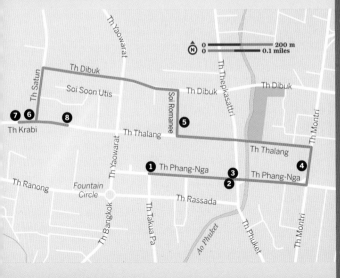

Best
Beaches

Ninety-nine percent of Phuket's six million annual visitors whiz straight to the beach – and no wonder why. Flashy developed strands mingle with hidden castaway paradises along the island's 49km west coast, where clear aqua waters lap gold-blonde sands fringed by lush jungle. Whatever your beach-bliss requirements, Phuket has it covered.

The Beach Scene

It's Phuket's west-coast beaches that lure travellers in. From the earthy, rocky coves of southern Rawai and that messy lust web, Hat Patong, to the gorgeous, discreet and increasingly popular northwest sands, Phuket's coastline contorts and twists into varied shapes and sizes, giving each stretch of sand its own rhythm. Since 2014, the Phuket beach clean-up operation has reduced beach services (and hassle) slightly, but on most beaches you'll find umbrellas and sun mats for rent, plus plenty of watersports. Chic beach clubs add glamour to swankier strands.

So Which Beach Is for You?

Most visitors make a beeline for the established, social tourist magnets of Hat Kata, Hat Karon and Hat Patong: long sandy swaths lined with resorts, restaurants, bars and every other facility you could ever need. If you'd prefer a more peaceful, secluded vibe, hunt down rocky coves off nondescript coastal roads between the main beaches, or head to Phuket's less touristed northwest coast. For five-star sparkle without the bustle, hit up Hat Surin and Ao Bang Thao.

Best for Families

Hat Kata Yai Two fun-filled crescent bays with good facilities and ideal for families. (p60)

Hat Karon Popular for its wide, squeaky white-sand stretch and space to spread out. (p60)

Hat Nai Han Nestled at the southern tip of the island, with a quiet local feel. (p75)

Hat Kamala Calm waters and good snorkelling at its northern end. (p85)

Best Hidden Sands

Hat Freedom Pristine beach a long-tail boat ride away from Patong's mayhem. (p44)

Hat Ya Nui A low-key sapphire Rawai bay backed by jungled

Boats at Hat Karon

mountains, with glorious sunsets. (p75)

Ao Sane This small boulder-strewn alabaster beach is a tucked-away Rawai secret. (p76)

Laem Singh A beautiful cape beach walled in by cliffs and without road access, north of Hat Kamala. (p85)

Best Water Activities

Hat Patong You name it, it's here. Diving, snorkeling, parasailing, jet skis and more. (p44)

Hat Kata Yai Excellent for surfing and good dive schools. (p60)

Hat Kamala Decent surf breaks and lovely for a snorkel. (p85)

Rawai Kitesurfing central on the east-coast beaches. (p76)

Hat Nai Yang Snorkelling in high season; surfing and kitesurfing during the monsoon. (p109)

Best Party Vibe

Hat Surin Beach-club chic mixed with a laid-back village feel. (p85)

Hat Bang Thao A beautiful 8km sweep of white sand with a couple of glitzy beach clubs. (p97)

Hat Patong Phuket's free-for-all party capital – go-go bars included. (p44)

Best for Relaxation

Hat Surin Stylish, stunning and unpretentious, Surin delivers the stress-relieving goods. (p85)

Hat Mai Khao Most of the time, you'll have Phuket's longest beach all to yourself. (p109)

Hat Nai Thon A quiet, peaceful strand with few distractions from its natural beauty. (p109)

Hat Kamala With its rustic, mellow vibe, Kamala is perfect for kicking back. (p85)

Hat Nai Yang Nature and tourism sit side by side on this laid-back national park strand. (p109)

Best
Dining

Beachfront dining, bamboo shacks, heaving markets, sizzling street grills and top-end resorts: Phuket makes for some seriously good eating. No matter where you do it, eating will be a huge part of your Phuket experience. All budgets, tastes and cuisines are catered for, with everything from freshly caught local seafood and red-hot Thai classics to 10-course degustation menus and home-style international comfort food.

High-End Dining

Most of Phuket's upmarket dining can be found in glitzy west-coast resorts, particularly along Hat Kata and Hat Surin. There are classy spots on the hill at the north end of Hat Patong, and some of Phuket's finest restaurants, with a modern urban twist, sit just outside the entrance to Laguna Phuket in Ao Bang Thao. The recent trend of fabulous beach clubs popping up all over the place has brought along more gourmet dining – and a lavish Sunday brunch craze. For those seeking some of Phuket's best food at more affordable prices, dining out in Phuket Town is a must.

Local Eats

To sample Phuket's sensational local-style food scene, head to Phuket Town. Tucked into the Old Town's character-filled Sino-Portuguese buildings are a number of generations-old eateries serving classic Thai and Phuketian fare. Across the island, find local markets for cheap, flavour-packed Thai treats.

Best Beachfront

Catch Gourmet buffets at a fashionable beach club. (p87)

Mom Tri's Kitchen Beautiful Hat Kata Noi views and fusion haute cuisine. (p64)

Taste The best of Surin's beachside urban-meets-surf eateries. (p87)

Bliss Beach Club Fantastic Thai-international dishes on a Bang Thao beach deck. (p98)

Best Splash-Out

Suay Exquisite fusion cuisine in a converted Phuket Town house. (p31)

Breeze Restaurant Understated east-coast surrounds and European-inspired dishes with Phuketian produce. (p105)

Food stalls at the Phuket Old Town Festival

ampot The latest rban-chic addition to ang Thao's culinary redentials. (p97)

lue Elephant Refined hai in a Sino-Portuguese huket Town mansion. 031)

oathouse Wine & Grill ea breezes and top-end ning at Kata's smartest staurant. (p64)

est Seafood

ang Rong Seafood ust-caught seafood on floating mangrove-haded deck. (p105)

aan Rimlay A superb awai beachside set-ng for fresh seafood. 079)

avoey One of the land's most popular eafood grills, in Patong. 48)

Best Local Thai

Pad Thai Shop Keeping it real in Karon, a no-frills *pàt tai* spot. (p64)

Raya Long-standing local fave in a Sino-Portuguese Phuket Town home. (p32)

The Orchids Popular for its classic Thai dishes, steps from Hat Patong. (p48)

Meena Restaurant Spicy Thai at a rustic sand-side Kamala shack. (p87)

Best Cafes

Gallery Cafe Wonderful, artsy all-day breakfast spot in Phuket Town. (p32)

Monkeypod Exceptional espresso and light lunches on Rte 4027. (p105)

Worth a Trip: Aziamendi

Southern Thailand's hottest new restaurant comes courtesy of three-Michelin-star Basque chef Eneko Atxa. Dining at avant-garde **Aziamendi** (083 006 5277; www.azia mendi.com; Iniala Beach House, 40/14 Mu 6, Ban Natai; 10-course tasting menu from 5300B; 6.30-9pm Tue-Sat Dec-Apr), 29km north of Phuket's airport, means ambitious, inventive 10-course tasting menus fusing Basque techniques with Thai flavours.

Best
Spas & Massage

Once you're done partying, paddling and sun lounging, it's time for some pampering. Soak, scrub, massage and wrap your way into beach bliss at any number of spas and massage points across Phuket. Splurge or save, depending on your needs. Brave a muscle-pounding Thai massage or go for a soothing floral body scrub and steam bath. The options are endless.

Choosing Your Spa

There seems to be a massage shop on every Phuket corner. Most are low-key family affairs where a traditional one-hour 300B Thai massage and a basic 200B mani-pedi are a real steal. The quality of service at these places varies and changes rapidly, as staff turnover is high. Go with your gut instinct or ask fellow travellers and hotel staff for local recommendations. No matter which spa you choose, a massage is still highly likely to be an extremely pleasant and relaxing experience.

If you fancy a more Western-style spa set-up, book into one of Phuket's plentiful resort spas. Though often affiliated with a glitzy hotel, most of these high-class affairs with sumptuous Zen designs, soft-voiced therapists and extensive treatment menus accept nonguests.

Where?

Phuket Town hosts some good-value lower-range spas. You'll find quality affordable massage parlours in Hat Patong, Hat Kata, Hat Surin, Phuket's northern beaches and Ao Bang Thao. The finest luxury spas are tucked into swanky resorts in Hat Kata, Hat Surin, Ao Bang Thao and the northern beaches, particularly Hat Mai Khao.

Best Indulgence

Sun Spa Treat yourself to a tamarind body polish at this sparkling luxury Surin spa. (p86)

Spa Royale Seaside treatment rooms and organic products at Kata's Mom Tri's Villa Royale. (p62)

Coqoon Spa A suspended 'nest suite', stunning rainforest surrounds and five-star treatment at Hat Nai Yang. (p110)

Baray Spa Kata sophistication: full-body coffee scrubs, gushing waterfalls and criss-crossing canals. (p60)

Baray Spa This ultramodern spa combines classic therapies with tech gadgets. Ah, the anti-jetlag pod... (p63)

st for Couples

a Luang Spa
uples' rooms overlook
us-filled ponds at this
gant Hat Mai Khao
sis. (p110)

n Spa Book the VIP
m for couples, featur-
a rose petal bath.
6)

a Spa Slick couples'
ms in private pebbled
rtyards on Hat Mai
o. (p110)

asana Spa You'll be
tled in a glass cube
cushy mats together
north Hat Patong.
6)

Best for Less

Raintree Spa Excellent-
value Phuket Town spa in
tranquil tropical gardens.
(p28)

Thai Carnation A real
local-vibe spa steal in
upmarket Ao Bang Thao.
(p97)

Mandarin Massage
Clean, cheap and cheer-
ful on Surin's main drag.
(p86)

Let's Relax A haven
from Patong's chaotic
streets, with a selection
of affordable treatments.
(p44)

Sovrana Spa All-natural
oils and reasonably
priced indulgent treat-
ments in Patong.
(p46)

Worth
a Trip:
Banyan Tree
Spa
If you're anywhere
near Ao Bang Thao,
don't miss the
highly regarded,
luxe **Banyan Tree
Spa** (📞076 372400;
www.banyantreespa.
com; 33 Mu 4, Th
Srisoonthorn, Laguna
Phuket; treatment
2900-7000B; ⏰8am-
9pm). Choose from
a wide selection of
Ayurveda- and yoga-
inspired treatments,
fruit-and-veg scrubs
(how about a carrot
purifier?) and Thai
massages. Or just
book in for the
whole day.

Best
For Romance

You'll spot loved-up couples everywhere on Phuket. When they're not strolling hand-in-hand along the sand or indulging in hours-long couples' massages, they're feeding each other fresh seafood at beachfront restaurants and snuggling together in dimly lit bars. Who can blame them, when Phuket dishes up romantic options at every other turn?

Beaches

You'll find some of Phuket's most pristine beaches on the northwest coast, with long white-sand stretches devoid of hordes of photo-snapping beach-goers – perfect for relaxing romantic walks. The southwest-coast sands are livelier, with beachfront bars and restaurants for intimate nights out. Phuket's craggy coastline conceals some exquisite viewpoints for watching the flaming-pink sun sink into the aqua Andaman Sea.

Spas

Sexy spas across the island welcome you for pampering treatments for two. Couples are well catered for, with private rooms where you can indulge in tailor-made two-person treatments such as aromatic baths, Thai massages and fruity scrubs. Some spas offer private beachfront couples' massages.

Beach Clubs

Exclusive beach clubs are Phuket's latest craze. Laze in beachfront infinity pools or on faux-leather loungers, dine on gourmet cuisine, sip exotic cocktails and feel fabulous all day long – without having to lift a finger.

Best Restaurants

Boathouse Wine & Gri Kata's classic 'special date' spot with beachsi dining and a lengthy wi list. (p64)

Suay A sultry fairy-lit garden in Phuket Town, with fantastic fusion foc for sharing. (p31)

Baan Rim Pa Plenty of candlelight and sea panoramas at this upmarket Thai winner. (p47)

Bliss Beach Club Dine under the stars overloc ing beautiful Ao Bang Thao. (p98)

Best Viewpoints

Laem Phromthep Cos up to your other half while watching the fire-ball sunset drop into th Andaman from Phuket southernmost point. (p72)

Laem Phromthep

ecret Viewpoint
cape Laem Phrom
ep's crowds and savour
e sunset here in peace.
75)

est Intimate Bars

mi Beach Club Sip
assy cocktails on swish
at Surin. (p89)

ka Bar Sway to reggae
eats at this rustic shack
the rocks on Hat Kata
i. (p66)

est Spas

in Spa Check into the
P couples' room for a
se-petal bath. (p86)

ua Luang Spa Gaze
ross lotus ponds as
erapists pummel your
cks in unison. (p110)

Best Beach Walks

Hat Bang Thao Escape
for a sunset stroll along
this divine 8km-long
white-sand stretch.
(p97)

Hat Mai Khao Walk for
hours without seeing
another soul on Phuket's
longest beach. (p109)

Best Activities

John Gray's Seacanoe
Float through hidden
lagoons on a twilight
kayak tour of Ao Phang-
Nga. (p30)

Phuket Heritage Trails
Wander the Old Town's
grand Sino-Portuguese
mansions with local
guides. (p27)

Worth a Trip: Cool Spa

Seek out **Cool Spa**
(☎ 076 371000; www.
coolspaphuket.com;
Sri Panwa, 88 Mu 8, Th
Sakdidej, Laem Phanwa,
Phuket; massages
2400-4000B; ⏰10am-
8.30pm), 12km south-
east of Phuket Town,
for fruit-infused
wraps, facials and
scrubs, ocean-view
pools and elegant,
intimate couples'
treatment rooms.
Post-massage,
laze on beanbags
at magical, sea-
surrounded, hilltop
Baba Nest (Sri
Panwa, 88 Mu 8, Th
Sakdidej; ⏰5-9pm)
lounge-bar.

Best
Places to Party

Most visitors come to Phuket for a party. Driftwood-clad beachside drinking shacks, classy lounge bars, heaving nightclubs and Patong's carnival of sin lure most people in. And, surprisingly, it isn't all about dirt-cheap shots and go-go bars: Phuket hosts blood-pumping Thai boxing, extravagantly theatrical cabaret and some of the Andaman's hottest clubs.

Best Clubs

Seduction Patong's slick, most popular party pad, with occasional global DJs. (p50)

Timber Hut A split-level Phuket Town pub-club loved by expats and Phuketians. (p34)

Illuzion A packed-out dancefloor and countless bars on Patong's Th Bangla. (p50)

Best Laid-Back Bars

Mr Pan's Art Space This friendly, eccentric Kata bar mixes drinks, art and...tattoos. (p67)

Comics Fun Phuket Town haunt to meet fashionable young Phuketians over live music. (p35)

After Beach Bar Perched high above Hat Kata Noi is this mellow Bob-Marley-fuelled bar. (p67)

Best Bars To Be Seen

Bimi Beach Club The baby of Surin's island-chic beach clubs, with upscale cocktails. (p89)

Bliss Beach Club Luxe Ao Bang Thao beach vibe and stylish Sunday parties. (p97)

Xana Beach Club Cabana cocktail lounging by day; pounding DJ sets by night. (p97)

Best Beachside Bars

Ska Bar A chilled-out reggae bar tucked into southern Hat Kata Yai. (p66)

Nikita's Feel the sea breeze on Hat Rawai, drink in hand and sand between your toes. (p80)

Sole Mio Enjoy the Hat Patong panorama over cocktails at this quirky pastel-painted bar. (p50)

Best Entertainmer

Phuket Simon Cabare This sensationally over-the-top trans cabaret is the quintessential Pator experience. (p52)

Bangla Boxing Stadiu Watch competitors battle it out with *moo-ay tai* (Thai boxing; also spelt *muay Thai*) bouts. (p52)

Patong Pub Crawl Hit Patong's Th Bangla for the ultimate debauched night out.

Best
Ways to Cure a Hangover

JORDAN SIEMENS / GETTY IMAGES ©

each holidays are synonymous with cocktails, eers and, well, more cocktails. You start late fternoon, sip some more cocktails at dinner nd, before you know it, you're on Th Bangla at am before groggily stumbling home. The next norning, the sun is shining, but this time it hurts, nd you're in desperate need of a good hangover ure.

Best Breakfasts

allery Cafe Number ne for pick-me-up uropean breakfasts fter bar-hopping around huket Town. (p32)

Breeze Restaurant Fall nto Phuket's lazy Sun-ay brunch scene sur-ounded by Laem Yamu's parkling seas. (p105)

German Bakery Rawai's o-to breakfast spot for elicious pastries, pan-akes and home-baked read. (p78)

Best Beach Clubs

Catch Beach Club ounge around on plush aybeds gazing out to Hat Surin. (p85)

Bliss Beach Club Soak p five-star service and nock back colourful cocktails on stunning Hat Bang Thao. (p97)

Re Ká Ta Beach Club Chill in the beachfront infinity pool or laze under umbrellas at this exclusive Kata hang out. (p62)

Bimi Beach Club Grab a Thai-jito and kick back in Surin style. (p89)

Best Coffee

Monkeypod Pick up Phuket's best coffee en route to the gibbons and a waterfall walk. (p105)

Bo(ok)hemian Sip gourmet lattes and flick through second-hand paperbacks overlook-ing Phuket Town's architecture. (p35)

Italian Job Liven up with a classic espresso before

a reinvigorating walk along Hat Kata. (p68)

Best Daytime Bars

After Beach Bar Power through with cold beers, flavour-popping *pàt tai* and spectacular Kata views. (p67)

Nikita's Let the sea breezes clear your head at this mellow Rawai fave. (p80)

Ska Bar Gaze across Hat Kata Yai and ease away aches with beers, cocktails and rasta beats. (p66)

Best Activities

Kata Hot Yoga Sweat and stretch it all out with 9am hot yoga. (p60)

Kite Zone Take to the waves to wash it all away with kitesurfing in Rawai. (p76)

Best
Diving & Snorkelling

Phuket enjoys an enviable central location relative to the Andaman's top diving destinations. The much-talked-about Similan Islands lie 100km northwest, while dozens of dive sites orbit Ko Phi-Phi and Ko Lanta, 40km and 72km southeast. Decent dive sites encircle Phuket, though these rank lower on the wow-o-meter. The best diving months are November to April.

Diving

Most operators frequent the nine sites orbiting Phuket, such as Ko Raya Yai (Ko Racha Noi and Ko Racha Yai). The reef off the southern tip of Raya Noi is the best spot, with soft corals and pelagic fish species aplenty, though it's for experienced divers. Manta and marble rays are frequently glimpsed here and, if you're lucky, whale sharks. One-day two-dive trips to nearby sites cost 3000B to 4000B.

Snorkelling

Snorkelling isn't wonderful off Phuket proper, though most resorts rent masks, snorkels and fins (per day 200B). You'll find better snorkelling (with greater visibility and variety of marine life) along the shores of small outlying islands, such as Ko Raya Yai and Ko Raya Noi.

In Patong

Sea Fun Divers Liveaboard dive trips to the Similan and Surin Islands, PADI courses and two- to three-dive day trips around Phuket and Ko Phi-Phi. Excellent service from keen, professional instructors. (p44)

Sea Bees This longstanding German-managed dive operation runs two-dive day trips to Ko Phi-Phi, Similans liveaboards and Open Water certification courses. (p46)

In Kata & Karon

Sunrise Divers The island's biggest liveaboard agent arranges a variety of two- and three-dive day trips, plus budget to luxury multiday trips to Ko Phi-Phi, the Similan and Surin Islands, and Myanmar's Mergui Archipelago. (p61)

Dive Asia Hits the standard southern-reef and Ko Phi-Phi day trips, and offers live-aboards to the Similan and Surin Islands. (p63)

Rumblefish Adventure Kata-based boutique dive school with the usual day trips, live-aboards and courses. (p62)

Best
Cultural
Experiences

LYNN GAIL / GETTY IMAGES ©

can be tricky to tear yourself away from
olicking about on the beach, but it's absolutely
orth the effort. Scattered across Phuket you'll
nd plenty of intriguing, well-worthy sights to
onnect you with the destination you're holiday-
g in. Phuket Town is the cultural heart of the
land, but each area has its own local flavour and
xperiences.

est Museums

**halang National
Museum** Standout
museum that unrav-
s Phuket's history
nd traces southern
hailand's ethnicities.
104)

**Phuket Thaihua
Museum** Phuket Town
eauty filled with exhibits
n Phuket's Chinese
nd tin-mining history.
p27)

Best Temples &
Shrines

Big Buddha One of the
world's biggest Buddha
tatues towers 45m high
top Phuket's Nakkerd
Hills. (p93)

Wat Phra Thong
Phuket's 'Golden Bud-
ha' is half buried; only
he head and shoulders
re visible. (p104)

**Shrine of the Serene
Light** Check out Taoist
etchings and vaulted
ceilings at this incense-
cloaked Phuket Town
shrine. (p25)

Wat Chalong Hugely
popular modern temple
with a spiritual vibration
and 36 golden Buddhas.
(p77)

Wat Suwan Khiri Wong
Yes, there's culture in
Patong, and it's a peace-
ful, elaborate working
wát. (p46)

Tsunami Memorial This
metallic, wave-inspired
work commemorates
those killed by the 2004
tsunami. (p85)

Best Architecture

Soi Romanee Phuket
Town's prettiest pastel-
painted street, packed

with revamped Sino-
Portuguese shophouses.

Chyn Pracha House
This beautifully pre-
served Sino-Portuguese
Phuket Town mansion is
one for antiques lovers.
(p27)

Best Cooking
Classes

Suay Cooking School
Fun, soulful, inventive
Phuket Town kitchen
sessions with one of
Phuket's top chefs.
(p27)

**Blue Elephant Cooking
School** Master Royal
Thai specialities in a re-
stored Sino-Portuguese
Phuket Town mansion.
(p28)

**Boathouse Cooking
Class** Fine-dining cook-
ing classes courtesy
of Kata's swankiest
restaurant. (p60)

Best
For Kids

There's loads for kids to do on Phuket. While the seedier side of Thailand's sex industry is on full show in Patong (we'd be reluctant to bring our kids here, though many people do), the rest of Phuket is fairly G-rated. Elephant rides are particularly plentiful on Phuket, but carry complex yet significant animal welfare concerns. For those with children who insist, ask around about more responsible outfits.

Best Restaurants

Crepes Village They'll love these sweet or savoury crepes in a fairy-lit Rawai garden. (p79)

Da Vinci Little ones get a playground while parents enjoy some peace at Rawai's favourite open-air Italian. (p78)

Bocconcino Creamy gelato served in cup or cone in this bright, cheery Surin cafe. (p88)

Bliss Beach Club Pool-splashing fun for kids and everyone else relaxes over cocktails on Hat Bang Thao. (p98)

Best Animal Action

Phuket Aquarium Plenty of underwater delights here, including tiger-striped catfish, reef sharks and a 600V electric eel. (p30)

Phuket Gibbon Rehabilitation Project This tiny sanctuary adopts captive gibbons in the hope they can be reintroduced to the wild. (p103)

Soi Dog Cavort with cats and dogs at this nonprofit animal-rescue foundation near Hat Mai Khao. (p109)

Best Activities

Phuket Riding Club Book ahead to trot through the luscious jungle around Rawai on horseback. (p76)

Kiteboarding Asia Adrenaline-addled older kids can tackle the Andaman's waves with kite-surfing in Rawai and Hat Nai Yang. (p110)

Khao Phra Thaew Royal Wildlife & Forest Reserve Head out to thi jungle-shrouded protected park full of waterfalls and singing gibbons (p103)

Nam Tok Bang Pae It's short jungle-shaded wall to these protected Khao Phra Thaew falls for a swim. (p104)

Best Theme Parks

Dino Park Mini-golf with a maze of caves, lagoons leafy gardens and dinosaur statues. (p63)

Splash Jungle Some se riously cool waterslides that are just perfect for kids bored of the beach. (p110)

Best
Boardriding

Water activities abound on Phuket – no surprise considering it's an island! The Andaman Sea a travellers' playground where you can sink underwater to discover a kaleidoscope of marine life while diving or snorkelling, fly high above on parasail or flit about its surface while surfing, kitesurfing, paddleboarding (SUP) or on a jet ski. Surfing, kitesurfing and SUP are fast becoming the most popular pursuits.

PAUL KENNEDY / GETTY IMAGES ©

Surfing

Phuket is an under-cover surf destination. The best waves arrive between June and September. South Hat Kata Yai (p60) is near one of the best breaks, topping out at 2m. Hat Nai Han (p75) gets bigger waves (up to 3m), in front of the yacht club. Both Kata and Nai Han have vicious undertows. Hat Kalim, north of Patong, is sheltered and has a consistent break of up to 3m. This is a hollow wave, and is considered the island's best break. The northernmost stretch of Hat Kamala (p85) has a nice 3m beach break. Sheltered Laem Singh (p85), 1km north, gets very big and fast. Hat Surin (p85) gets some of Phuket's most challenging waves. Hat Nai Yang (p109) has a consistent (if soft) wave that breaks more than 200m offshore. In low season, most of these beaches rent surfboards (per hour 250B to 300B).

Kitesurfing

One of the world's fastest-growing sports is also one of Phuket's latest addictions. The best kitesurfing spots are Hat Nai Yang (p109; (April to October) and Rawai (p76; mid-October to March). All listed kitesurfing outfitters are affiliated with the International Kite-boarding Organization (www.ikointl.com).

Best Surfing

Phuket Surf A great source of surfing info with lessons and board rental on Hat Kata Yai. (p62)

Hat Kamala Monsoon-season board hire and surfing classes (1500B). (p85)

Best Kitesurfing & Stand-Up Paddle (SUP)

Kite Zone Courses ranging from one-hour tasters to three-day sessions, plus SUP trips. (p76)

Kiteboarding Asia Large-scale school based on Hat Nai Yang; also offers lessons off Rawai's Hat Friendship. (p110)

Best
For a Rainy Day

We all pray for sunny skies when booking that beach holiday, but the reality is that in tropical paradises, such as Phuket, sudden downpours can drench you without warning and have you racing away from the beach, then twiddling your thumbs about what to do next. Fortunately, Phuket comes prepared with plenty of wet-weather entertainment.

Best Shopping

Jung Ceylon Yes, it's a shopping centre, but that means plenty of cash-splashing opportunities for rainy days. (p54)

Lemongrass House Gorgeous store with a Phuket-grown range of all-natural beauty products. (p90)

Ban Boran Textiles Sift though piled-high shelves of raw silk, cotton clothes and jewellery in Phuket Town. (p36)

Chandra Stock up on beach-chic fashion in preparation for sunnier Surin days. (p90)

Best Spas

Spa Royale Hear the waves crashing from your seaside Kata treatment room while enjoying a cucumber wrap. (p62)

Let's Relax Indulge indoors in Patong with steam baths and soothing, affordable massages. (p44)

The Spa While it's wet outside, delight in a red-wine scrub at one of Karon's most ambient spas. (p62)

Coqoon Spa With these northern rainforest surrounds, the rain will make your massage even more refreshing. (p110)

Best Cooking Classes

Pum Thai Cooking School Heat things up with fiery curries and 'Little Wok' classes at Patong's Pum Thai. (p46)

Blue Elephant Cooking School You'll barely notice the rain at this splendid cooking-school mansion. (p28)

Boathouse Cooking Class Keep dry while learning culinary secrets from one of the island's top chefs. (p60)

Best Museums

Thalang National Museum Dig deep into Phuket's fascinating history at this top-notch museum. (p104)

Phuket Thaihua Museum Flashy museum packed with historical displays for waiting it out in Phuket Town. (p27)

Chyn Pracha House A Sino-Portuguese mansion that lets you peek into Phuket Town's history. (p27)

Best
Guys' Getaways

MATTHEW WAKEM / GETTY IMAGES ©

Best Adventure

Nicky's Handlebar Take some Harleys for a lap or join a big-beast bike full-day trip to Phang-Nga Province, before hitting the bike-themed bar. (p45)

Cable Jungle Adventure Phuket Zip-line 300m between ancient ficus trees through the lush jungles of Thalang. (p105)

Rawai Supa Muay Thai Get competitive with a few Thai boxing bouts at this champion-founded training camp for Thais and travellers. (p75)

Kite Zone Grab your kites and fly across the waves with adrenaline-filled kitesurfing sessions off Rawai and Hat Nai Yang. (p76)

Amazing Bike Tours Speed off on a half-day cycling tour through Khao Phra Thaew Royal Wildlife & Forest Reserve or jump on a day trip to pretty Ko Yao Noi. (p61)

Best Bars & Clubs

Rockin' Angels Chug cheap beer and listen to rockin' tunes with Phuketians and expats in Phuket Town. (p35)

Flip Side Live out the craft beer and burger dream in laid-back Hat Rawai. (p81)

Boat Bar Swing by for glitzy trans cabarets and dance-club beats at Patong's original gay nightspot. (p50)

Ska Bar Meet fellow travellers at this casual Hat Kata Yai reggae bar with Thai bartenders, fire shows and killer sundowners. (p66)

Laguna Rawai Party late into the weekend nights at this multi-bar and club complex. (p81)

Best Entertainment

Pub Crawl Patong Hit pounding Th Bangla on this pub-and-grub crawl through the heart of Patong.

Bangla Boxing Stadium Watch competitive *moo·ay tai* boxers, both Thai and foreign, go head-to-head in Patong. (p52)

Phuket Shooting Range Complex Choose from shooting, go-karting, archery and paintball at this sprawling activity complex in Rawai. (p77)

Best Shopping

Metal Art A quirky Patong gallery packed with sci-fi robot sculptures and motorcycles made from scrap metal car parts. (p55)

Drawing Room Abstract modern canvases and a street-art vibe in Phuket Town. (p37)

Best
Girls' Getaways

Best Pampering

Bua Luang Spa Luxury indulgence at one of Hat Mai Khao's most serene spas. (p110)

Spa Royale Treat yourselves to apple polisher baths in elegant Kata seaside surrounds. (p62)

Sun Spa Relax with toning 'Qi Gong' facials at this decadent Surin spa. (p86)

Raintree Spa Keep things tropical with two-hour 'fruit salad' scrubs in Phuket Town. (p28)

Let's Relax A reliable, great-value, eucalyptus-infused Patong day spa. (p44)

Best Shopping

Lemongrass House All-natural beauty products, scented soaps and tropical shampoos in Surin. (p90)

Ranida Peek past antique Buddhas to vintage-inspired couture clothing at this Phuket Town boutique. (p36)

Chandra Breezy beach-glam dresses and embroidered bikinis make this Surin boutique a favourite. (p90)

Baru Floaty dresses, flowy kaftans and skimpy bikinis in Kata and Patong. (p52)

Ban Boran Textiles Pick up silk scarves, linen clothing and unique jewellery in Phuket Town. (p36)

Best Beach Clubs

Re Ká Ta Beach Club Lounge around the beachfront infinity pool, cocktail in hand, on Hat Kata Yai. (p62)

Xana Beach Club Party-vibe cabanas on a sensational sweep of Ao Bang Thao sand. (p97)

Catch Beach Club Sprawl under your personal umbrella with a bottle of bubbly. (p85)

Bliss Beach Club Flit from pool to Andaman Sea at this luxurious Ao Bang Thao hang-out. (p97)

Best Bars

Bimi Beach Club Stylish Surin beach-club bar, perfect for a girls' night out. (p89)

After Beach Bar Take in the stunning clifftop views over cheap drinks at this Kata bamboo bar. (p67)

Best Activities

Kata Hot Yoga Fold and twist into your happiest holiday selves at this sweltering studio. (p60)

Kite Zone Zip across the Nai Yang or Rawai waves mastering kitesurfing. (p76)

Blue Elephant Cooking School One of Phuket's finest restaurants teaches you its much-sought-after secrets. (p28)

Survival Guide

Survival Guide

Before You Go

When to Go

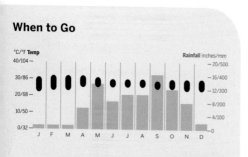

°C/°F Temp
40/104 —
30/86 —
20/68 —
10/50 —
0/32 —

Rainfall inches/mm
— 20/500
— 16/400
— 12/300
— 8/200
— 4/100
— 0

J F M A M J J A S O N D

➡ **Low Season (May–Oct)** Slashed prices, fewer crowds, plenty of sunshine mixed with torrential downpours, and the vibrant Vegetarian Festival in October.

➡ **Peak Season (Dec–Jan)** Blue skies mean soaring prices. Book all accommodation, high-end restaurants and transport well in advance.

➡ **Shoulder Season (Nov & mid-Jan–Mar)** Still some crowds, but without peak rates. Weather is a good bet, with calm seas.

Book Your Stay

☑ **Top Tip** During high season it can be impossible to find a room. Book well ahead over Christmas, New Year and Songkran.

➡ Phuket accommodation is generally pricier than across the rest of Thailand.

➡ Phuket prices are determined by seasons; the low season sees rates drop by 40% to 60%.

➡ There are hundreds of places to sleep on Phuket, from social, no-frills hostels to smart midrange hotels, swanky self-catering apartments, zenned-out villas and exquisite five-star resorts.

➡ When choosing where to stay, work out whether you want to be in the heart of pumping nightlife in Patong; somewhere more laid-back but with all the facilities, such as Karon, Kata or Kamala; somewhere far away from

, such as the north-
beaches; or in the
nd's cultural capital,
ket Town.

ful Websites

oda (www.agoda.
n) Listings, good mid-
ge deals; sometimes
only booking option.

uket.com (www.
uket.com) Recom-
ndations; online
king; good info on the
nd.

nie's Phuket (www.
ie-monk.blogspot.
n) Tips and reviews
m a long-time Phuket
gger.

ely Planet (www.
elyplanet.com/
uket) Author recom-
ndations, traveller
um, booking engine.

t Budget

Top Tip It's getting
tty difficult to find
thing under 1000B in
ong and Kata during
November-to-April
n season, but Phuket
vn is a treasure trove
affordable lodging.

ota Hostel (www.
tahostel.com) Warm,
dern posh-tel pad
h smartish well-

equipped dorms, 100m
from Patong's Th Bangla.

Fantasy Hill Bungalow
(fantasyhill@hotmail.
com) Longstanding
peaceful and central
Kata bungalows, tucked
into a lush hillside
garden.

**Patong Backpacker
Hostel** (www.phuket
backpacker.com) Great
location near Hat Patong
and its bars, with social,
quality, good-value
dorms.

Ai Phuket (www.ai
phukethostel.com)
Bright muralled dorms
pack out this character-
ful Phuket Town hostel.

Pineapple Guesthouse
(www.pineapple
phuket.com) Excellent
Thai-English-run budget
spot in Karon, with bril-
liantly kept, if simple,
modern rooms.

Good 9 at Home
(www.facebook.com/
good9athome) Feature
walls spice up small but
wonderfully fresh, gleam-
ing, contemporary-style
digs in Rawai.

Best Midrange

The RomManee (www.
therommanee.com) Four

quirky-chic 'boutique
guesthouse' rooms
in a restored Sino-
Portuguese Phuket
Town shophouse.

Baipho (www.baipho.
com) Outrageously arty
Patong guesthouse filled
with Buddha imagery,
modern art and urban
touches.

Papa Crab (www.phuket
papacrab.com) Classy,
homey and discreet
with a boutique twist in
Kamala.

Bazoom Haus (www.
bazoomhostel.com) Pol-
ished concrete, DJ decks
and recessed lighting
make for a comfy, stylish
Karon choice.

Casa Blanca (www.
casablancaphuket.com)
Spanish-themed pastel-
and-white touches in
an elegantly revamped
Sino-Portuguese Phuket
Town home.

Sabai Corner (www.
facebook.com/Sabai-Cor
ner-150517525037992)
Isolated, independent
concrete studios enjoy
fabulous 270-degree
ocean views between
Kata and Rawai.

Best Top End
☑ **Top Tip** Most advertised top-end hotel rates exclude compulsory 7% government sales tax and 10% service charge; it's tacked on at charging time.

Point Yamu by Como
(www.comohotels.com) Coolly contemporary five-star stunner incorporating Thai influences, all-engulfing sea vistas and blue-on-blue private-pool rooms.

Sri Panwa (www.
sripanwa.com) Beautifully decadent resort on secluded Laem Phanwa, with multi-pool villas, private pools and the dreamiest of views.

BYD Lofts (www.
bydlofts.com) Luxurious urban-chic apartments, some with private pools, minutes from Hat Patong.

Twin Palms (www.
twinpalms-phuket.com) Sleek contemporary Hat Surin resort with a maze of pools and a sensational spa.

Anantara Layan (www.
anantara.com) An oasis of elegant, understated luxury hidden on its own

wild-feel bay, just north of Ao Bang Thao.

Sawasdee Village (www.
phuketsawasdee.com) Opulent Kata spa resort with gorgeously ornate Thai-Moroccan bungalows immersed in tropical gardens.

Arriving in Phuket

☑ **Top Tip** For the best way to get to your accommodation, see p17

From Phuket International Airport
Most visitors arrive into **Phuket International Airport** (Map p108; ☏ 076 327230; www.phuketairport thai.com), 30km northwest of Phuket Town, on direct international flights or via Bangkok. From here, it takes 45 minutes to an hour to reach the southern beaches, where most people stay.

➡ **Metered taxis** Located 50m to the right as you exit airport arrivals. By meter, including a 100B 'airport tax', you'll pay no more than 700B to anywhere on the island from the airport. Confirm

use of meter before heading off.

➡ **Private taxi** Easiest tion to your hotel, cost 500B to 1200B, depending on your destination

➡ **Minibus** Shared minibuses (minimum people) to Patong (per person 180B), Karon (person 200B) and Kat (200B).

➡ **Bus** Hourly bright-orange government air port bus (www.airport busphuket.com) to Phuket Town (100B, or hour, 6.30am to 8.30p via the Heroines Monument. Not an option if you're staying at the beach.

➡ **Car hire** Very conven ent way to get around t island. **Avis** (☏ 02 251 11 www.avis.com; ⏲ 7am-9p and **Hertz** (☏ 076 32854 www.hertz.com; ⏲ 8am-9pm) have airport office Rental from 1200B per day.

From Tha Rassad (Rassada Pier)
Phuket's Tha Rassada, 3km southeast of Phuk Town, is the main pier for boats to Ko Phi-Phi, Krabi, Ao Nang, Ko Lan the Trang Islands, Ko Li and even as far as Pula

gkawi (Malaysia).
itional services to
bi and Ao Nang via the
ao islands leave from
Bang Rong, 26km
h of Tha Rassada.

m Phuket Bus
rminals 1 & 2

rstate buses arrive
and depart from
ket Bus Terminal
Thepkrasattri), 4km
th of Phuket Town.
erwise, if you're on an
con minibus, you'll be
pped at either one of
main beaches or at
ket Bus Terminal 1
Phang-Nga), in Phuket
n.

etting
round

al Phuket transport
errible. The systems
lace make tour-
either stay on their
sen beach, rent a car
motorbike, or take
erpriced taxis or túk-
. That said, thanks to
recent crackdown on
ket's 'taxi mafia', the
anglehold local drivers
e enjoyed may be
ning to an end.

Private Taxi

☑ **Best for...** independence and comfort, without self-driving.

➡ Air-conditioned car and driver, booked through most travel agenices and resorts, costs around 1500B for eight hours.

➡ Works well for travellers in a group, who can split costs and get around easily.

Sŏrng·tǎa·ou (Passenger Pick-Up Truck)

☑ **Best for...** budget travel and keeping it local.

➡ These open-sided minibuses run from Phuket Town to most beaches (25B to 40B) from about 7am to 5pm.

➡ To get from one beach to another (say Hat Surin to Hat Patong), you'll often have to go via Phuket Town, which takes hours.

Túk-Túk

☑ **Best for...** beach-to-beach travel and short trips within town.

➡ Not the three-wheeler túk-túk you'll find elsewhere in Thailand, these red open-air minivans are based in all towns.

➡ Use for local trips; popular but pricey way to get between beaches.

➡ Costs around 200B for shorter trips around town, 300B between Kata and Karon, and 500B for longer journeys (eg Kata to Patong). Bargain hard, but don't expect prices to drop much.

Scooter/ Motorcycle

☑ **Best for...** independent, budget-conscious travel; exploring off-road nooks.

➡ The most cost-effective way to get around.

➡ Riding a motorbike on Phuket can be hazardous. Know the risks, wear a helmet and be careful driving at night.

➡ Rental from beachtown road-side stalls costs 250B to 300B per day, but rarely includes insurance.

➡ You'll often be asked to leave your passport as guarantee; a photocopy should be fine.

➡ There are motorbike taxis in Phuket Town and Patong, with greenvested riders who do local trips for 30B.

Car Hire

☑ **Best for...** independent, in-depth explorations.

→ Being behind the wheel in Thailand might sound like madness, but driving on Phuket isn't so bad. Traffic is manageable, roads are wide and roundabouts are easy to manoeuvre.

→ Drive on the left-hand side of the road.

→ Suzuki jeeps and Toyota Sedans cost from 1200B per day (including insurance and GPS).

→ In low season, rates can drop to 800B. If you hire for over three days, rates are reduced even more.

→ **Pure Car Rent** (📞076 211002; www.purecarrent. com; 75 Th Rassada; ⊙8am-7pm) is a reliable Phuket Town rental company with good prices. Airport-

based **Avis** (📞02 251 1131; www.avis.com; ⊙7am-9pm) and **Hertz** (📞076 328545; www.hertz.com; ⊙8am-9pm) offer decent deals too.

Boat

☑ **Best for...** island-hopping and sea breezes.

→ Wooden long-tail boats are the most commonly hired vessel for visiting surrounding islands, but speedboats are increasingly popular. Both are available from many of the beaches.

→ Rawai is one of the best places to charter boats to neighbouring islands year-round, including Ko Bon (long-tail/speedboat 1200/2400B) and Coral Island (1800/3500B).

→ From Kata, full- and half-day charters head to Ko Bon and Coral Island for around 5000B; you'll

save some baht if you by land to Rawai first.

→ From Patong, Hat Fre dom, just southwest, is popular day trip (1500 return, 15 minutes).

Essential Informatio

Business Hours

☑ **Top Tip** Opening ho can vary a lot, especiall during low season. Ask around if possible.

Restaurants Mostly op for breakfast from arou 8am and close by 11pm

Shops and businesse Open approximately 9a to 7pm in Phuket Town and 10am to as late as 11pm in beach resort areas.

Banks Open 9.30am to 3.30pm Monday to Friday.

Temples Generally ope by 8am and until 6pm.

Pubs and bars Open from around 11am to midnight or later.

Cafes Open approximately 8am to 10pm.

Money-Saving Tips

→ The best Phuket deals emerge during low season, when hotels and car-hire agencies slash rates by 40% to 60%.

→ Hunt down cheap and delicious food at street stalls, markets and humble local-style joints.

→ Hiring a motorbike or car is the most economical transport option for exploring the island.

→ Book midrange and high-end accommodation several months ahead for good deals.

7-Elevens Stay open hours, as do other convenience stores.

Electricity

220V/50Hz

220V/50Hz

Discounts

If you're visiting during low season, you'll get 40% to 60% off most accommodation (from five-star resorts to backpacker favourites), plus discounts on diving trips and car rental

Emergencies

Bangkok Hospital Phuket (☎076 254425; www.phukethospital.com; Th Hongyok Uthit)

Fire ☎199

Phuket International Hospital (☎076 361818, 076 249400; www.phuket internationalhospital.com; 44 Th Chalermprakiat)

Police (☎076 212046, 191; Th Chumphon)

Tourist Police (☎1669, 076 342719; cnr Th Thawiwong & Th Bangla)

Money

☑ **Top Tip** Small local-style establishments, operators and drivers rarely have change for 1000B notes. Break them at your hotel or with large vendors instead.

Currency The basic unit of Thai currency is the baht (B), made up of 100 satang. Notes come in 20B, 50B, 100B, 500B and 1000B. Coins are valued at 1B, 2B, 5B and 10B.

ATMs These are everywhere, including the airport and most 7-Elevens. Thai ATMs now charge a 180B foreign-transaction fee. It's worth notifying your bank that you'll be travelling to Thailand.

Credit cards Widely accepted.

Money changers Common for those needing to exchange foreign currency; also at the airport.

Tipping At most upmarket eateries a 10% service charge is added to your bill. Elsewhere, service staff always appreciate a tip of 5% to 10%.

Public Holidays

New Year's Day 1 January

Chinese New Year (lunar) January to March

Magha Puja (lunar) January to March

Chakri Day 6 April

Songkran (lunar) April

Coronation Day 5 May

Visakha Puja (lunar) May

Asalha Puja (lunar) July

Khao Phansa (lunar) July

Queen's Birthday
12 August

Chulalongkorn Day
23 October

King's Birthday
5 December

Constitution Day
10 December

Safe Travel

Considering the number of tourists and the volume of cash spent on Phuket, it's a pretty safe place. You'll rarely feel uncomfortable or guarded, even in wild Patong. However, like most places in the world, violence and crime do happen on the outskirts, especially late at night.

During the May-to-October monsoon, fierce undertows make Phuket's beaches dangerous and dozens of drownings occur every year. Red flags are posted on beaches when the undercurrents are strong; don't swim if they're flying. If you do get caught in a rip tide, don't fight it by swimming back to the beach. Instead, swim parallel to shore and you will eventually elude the rip's grasp. Remember to keep an eye out for jet skis, long-tails and parasailers when swimming.

Be aware of unscrupulous operators in the main beach areas, particularly Patong. Jet-ski owners are infamous for scamming tourists into paying for pre-existing damage to the jet ski's underbody. Scooter owners have been known to try similar things. Make a condition report by taking photos to avoid unpleasantries.

Random sexual assaults on women can happen. Think twice before sunbathing topless (a big no-no in Thailand anyway) or alone, especially on isolated beaches.

Telephone

Mobile Phones

➡ The easiest phone option for Phuket is a mobile phone with a prepaid local SIM card, ideally with a data package. You can buy mobile phones at shopping centres, 7-Elevens and smaller phone stores. If you already have a SIM-unlocked phone that supports the GSM network, just buy a Thai SIM card (with an assigned phone number and some prepaid credit), then pa

---

Dos & Don'ts

Royal Family The royal family is much beloved, so never disrespect them, which can cause serious offence and result in jail time.

Drugs Be aware of strict rules for drug possession.

Saving Face An important etiquette rule: avoid public displays of anger or impatience.

Etiquette Don't point your feet directly at people.

Temples Always remove your shoes at temples and dress modestly, covering knees and shoulders.

Public Affection Displays of public affection are taboo.

you go. Convenience
res sell SIM cards and
ups. Otherwise, it's
aming rates on your
me-country phone
n. Whatever phone
're using, wi-fi is wide-
available at cafes, bars,
tels and restaurants.

one Codes

ailand country code
66

uket area code 📞 076

ilets

e bulk of toilets you'll
counter in Phuket will
Western sit-down
le, but local places
ay have squat toilets.

urist Information

mediately east of
ntral Phuket Town,
urism Authority of
ailand (TAT; 📞 076
036; www.tourismthailand.
/Phuket; 191 Th Thalang;
8.30am-4.30pm) is

particularly helpful on
Phuket Town, but also has
maps and information
on activities across the
island and surrounding
area.

Travellers with Disabilities

➡ Given the narrow
footpaths, chaotic traffic
and very few adaptations
(such as ramps) on its
streets and transport
systems, Phuket can
prove tricky for travellers
with disabilities.

➡ Many hotels lack lifts,
especially in the budget
category.

➡ If you travel with a
friend who can help you
navigate the street may-
hem, however, you'll have
no trouble at all.

➡ If you are disabled and
plan on travelling solo,
your best bet is to hire
a car with a driver who

will get you wherever you
want to go safely.

➡ Lonely Planet's free
Accessible Travel guide
can be downloaded here:
http://lptravel.to/
AccessibleTravel

Visas

➡ Most Western nationals
arriving by air will be
granted a free 30-day
visa.

➡ Check with the **Min-**
istry of Foreign Affairs
(www.mfa.go.th) or your
nearest Thai embassy on
whether you must apply
for a visa before arriving
in Phuket.

➡ The **Phuket Immigra-**
tion Office (📞 076 221905;
www.phuketimmigration.go.th;
482 Th Phuket; ⏱ 8.30am-
4.30pm Mon-Fri) deals with
visa extensions.

Language

In Thai the meaning of a syllable may be altered by means of tones. Standard Thai has five tones: low (eg *bàht*), mid (eg *dee*), falling (eg *mâi*), high (eg *máh*) and rising (eg *săhm*). The range of all five tones is relative to each speaker's vocal range, so there is no fixed 'pitch' intrinsic to the language.

Read our pronunciation guides as if they were English and you'll be understood. The hyphens indicate syllable breaks; some syllables are divided with a dot to help you pronounce compound vowels (eg *mêu·a·raí*). Note that **b** is a hard 'p' sound, almost like a 'b' (eg in 'hip-bag') and **d** is a hard 't' sound, like a sharp 'd' (eg in 'mid-tone').

To enhance your trip with a phrase-book, visit **lonelyplanet.com**. Lonely Planet iPhone phrasebooks are available through the Apple App store.

Basics

Hello.	สวัสดี	sà-wàt-dee
Goodbye.	ลาก่อน	lah gòrn
Yes./No.	ใช่/ไม่	châi/mâi
Please.	ขอ	kŏr
Thank you.	ขอบคุณ	kòrp kun
Excuse me.	ขออภัย	kŏr à-pai
Sorry.	ขอโทษ	kŏr tôht

How are you?
สบายดีไหม　　sà-bai dee măi

Fine. And you?
สบายดีครับ/ค่ะ　sà-bai dee kráp/
แล้วคุณล่ะ　　kâ láa·ou kun lâ (m/f)

Do you speak English?
คุณพูดภาษา　　kun pôot pah-săh
อังกฤษได้ไหม　ang-grìt dâi măi

I don't understand.
ผม/ดิฉันไม่　　pŏm/dì-chăn mâi
เข้าใจ　　　　kôw jai (m/f)

Eating & Drinking

I'd like (the menu), please.
ขอ (รายการ　　kŏr (rai gahn
อาหาร) หน่อย　ah-hăhn) nòy

I don't eat ...
ผม/ดิฉัน　　　pŏm/dì-chăn
ไม่กิน ...　　　mâi gin ... (m/f)

eggs	ไข่	kài
nuts	ถั่ว	tòo·a
red meat	เนื้อแดง	néu·a daang

That was delicious!
อร่อยมาก　　à-ròy mâhk

Cheers!
ไชโย　　　　chai-yoh

Please bring the bill.
ขอบิลหน่อย　kŏr bin nòy

Shopping

I'd like to buy ...
อยากจะซื้อ ...　yàhk jà séu ...

How much is it?
เท่าไร　　　　tôw-rai

at's too expensive.

งไป paang bai

n you lower the price?

ราคาได้ไหม lót rah-kah dâi măi

mergencies

lp! ช่วยด้วย chôo·ay dôo·ay

away! ไปให้พ้น bai hâi pón

ll a doctor!

กหมอหน่อย rêe·ak mŏr nòy

ll the police!

กตำรวจหน่อย rêe·ak đam·ròo·at nòy

ill.

/ดิฉัน pŏm/dì-chăn

ย bòo·ay (m/f)

lost.

/ดิฉัน pŏm/dì-chăn

งทาง lŏng tahng (m/f)

ere are the toilets?

งน้ำอยู่ที่ไหน hôrng nám yòo têe năi

me & Numbers

at time is it?

มงแล้ว gèe mohng láa·ou

rning	เช้า	chów
ernoon	บ่าย	bài
ening	เย็น	yen
sterday	เมื่อวาน	mêu·a wahn
day	วันนี้	wan née
morrow	พรุ่งนี้	prûng née

1	หนึ่ง	nèung
2	สอง	sŏrng
3	สาม	săhm
4	สี่	sèe
5	ห้า	hâh
6	หก	hòk
7	เจ็ด	jèt
8	แปด	bàat
9	เก้า	gôw
10	สิบ	sìp

Transport & Directions

Where's ...?

... อยู่ที่ไหน ... yòo têe năi

What's the address?

ที่อยู่คืออะไร têe yòo keu à-rai

Can you show me (on the map)?

ให้ดู (ในแผนที่) hâi doo (nai păn têe)

ได้ไหม dâi măi

When's the first bus?

รถเมล์คันแรก rót mair kan râak

มาเมื่อไร mah mêu·a rai

A (one-way/return) ticket, please.

ขอตั๋ว (เที่ยว kŏr đŏo·a (tèe·o

เดียว/ไปกลับ). dee·o/bai glàp)

Does it stop at ...?

รถจอดที่ ... ไหม rót jòrt têe ... măi

I'd like to get off at ...

ขอลงที่ ... kŏr long têe ...

Index

See also separate subindexes for:

🟦 Eating p156

🟤 Drinking p156

🟢 Entertainment p157

🟧 Shopping p157

Behind the Scenes

Send Us Your Feedback

We love to hear from travellers – your comments help make our books better. We read every word, and we guarantee that your feedback goes straight to the authors. Visit **lonelyplanet.com/contact** to submit your updates and suggestions.

Note: We may edit, reproduce and incorporate your comments in Lonely Planet products such as guidebooks, websites and digital products, so let us know if you don't want your comments reproduced or your name acknowledged. For a copy of our privacy policy visit lonelyplanet.com/privacy.

Isabella's Thanks

Thanks to everyone who helped out on the road, whether knowingly or not, particularly Jamie Monk and Lee Cobaj for Phuket intel, elephant-expert John Roberts, the Gibbon Rehab Project crew, Wiwan for emergency assistance and Ann for Thai language tips. Extra special thanks to Andrew, Raquel and Papi, and to my favourite research assistant, Jack Noble.

Acknowledgments

Cover photograph: Sunset over Phuket/ Travel Pix Collection/AWL

This Book

This 4th edition of Lonely Planet's *Pocket Phuket* guidebook was researched and written by Isabella Noble. The previous edition was researched and written by Trent Holden and Kate Morgan. This guidebook was produced by the following:

Destination Editor Sarah Reid **Product Editors** Alison Ridgway, Tracy Whitmey **Regional Senior Cartographer** Diana von Holdt **Book Designer** Michael Buick **Coordinating Editor** Kristin Odijk **Assisting Editor** Kate Evans **Cover Researcher** Naomi Parker

Thanks to Daniel Corbett, Bruce Evans, Nida Karnkorkul, Luna Soo, Lauren Wellicome

Our Writer

Isabella Noble

English-Australian-Spanish Isabella writes about Thailand, India, Spain and beyond for Lonely Planet, *Telegraph Travel* and others. A big fan of Phuket despite its touristy reputation (she also penned the Phuket & the Andaman Coast chapter of Lonely Planet's *Thailand* and *Thailand's Islands & Beaches*), Isabella first fell for the Andaman on a 2008 backpacking extravaganza. Her highlights this time around: boating into gorgeous Ko Ngai, getting lost in colourful Phuket Town, finally tackling tubing in Khao Sok and escaping it all on Ko Phayam. She lives in London and blogs at www.isabella noble.blogspot.com. Find her on Twitter and Instagram (@isabellamnoble).

Published by Lonely Planet Publications
ABN 36 005 607 983
4th edition – Jul 2016
ISBN 978 1 74321 758 0
© Lonely Planet 2016   Photographs © as indicated 2016
10 9 8 7 6 5 4 3 2 1
Printed in China